in the presence of
spirits

About the Author

Barbara Parks (Kalamunda, Western Australia) is a micro-biologist and podiatrist with her own private practice. She has spoken about poltergeists on the radio and is frequently sought out for paranormal investigations. She lives in Australia with her husband and three children.

BARBARA PARKS

in the presence of
spirits

a true story of ghostly visitations

Llewellyn Publications
Woodbury, Minnesota

FIRST EDITION
First Printing, 2012

Book design by Donna Burch
Cover art © : Woman: iStockphoto.com/Ivan Bliznetsov
                Grunge border: iStockphoto.com/Duncan Walker
                Picture frame: iStockphoto.com/Erkki Makkonen
Cover design by Kevin R. Brown
Editing by Andrea Neff
Interior photographs provided by the author

Llewellyn Publications is a registered trademark of Llewellyn Worldwide Ltd.

Library of Congress Cataloging-in-Publication Data
Parks, Barbara, 1969–
  In the presence of spirits : a true story of ghostly visitations /
by Barbara Parks. — 1st ed.
      p.   cm.
  ISBN 978-0-7387-3352-4
1. Parks, Barbara, 1969– 2. Clairvoyants—Biography.
3. Parapsychology—Biography. I. Title.
  BF1283.P375A3 2012
  133.9'1092—dc23
  [B]

                                                    2012012826

Llewellyn Publications
A Division of Llewellyn Worldwide Ltd.
2143 Wooddale Drive
Woodbury, MN 55125-2989
www.llewellyn.com

Printed in the United States of America

Dedication

For Stuart
and our three darlings:
Eloise, Claire, and Daniel

Acknowledgments

First and foremost, thanks go to my parents, Luka and Marica, and my siblings, Duro, Vlasta, and Luka, with whom I shared the Kensington days. Whoever would have thought that something so wonderful would come of what were the most frightening of times? Thank you for sharing my journey.

Thank you, Luka, for reminding me of the crane incident and other snippets I had forgotten, and for letting me lug a mattress into your room and sleep on your floor when I was feeling scared. You always were much braver than I!

Extra thanks to you, Vla, for brandishing your red pen and exercising your astute editorial skills on my early drafts. You never fail to impress me.

Thank you, Michael, for allowing me to share the account of our trip to Albany, and in particular for graciously tolerating my mirth at your expense. I still can't stop smiling whenever I think about it!

Amy Glaser, my editor and long-distance friend, thank you for helping shape my book into something to be proud of!

Heartfelt thanks to Andrea Neff and all the team at Llewellyn. Your friendly professionalism has enriched my experience of working on this book.

To my beautiful friends Chris and Bert, I thank you for everything. You know why!

To Mick, Olga, and Dennyne, with much love and thanks for letting me share Deni's story.

Special thanks to everyone who has allowed me to share their stories within these pages. I'm especially grateful to those of you who have allowed me to relate your loved ones' post-death visits. These experiences have immeasurably enriched my life and I am so grateful to have your permission to share them. Much love to you all.

And finally, I give heartfelt thanks to my beautiful family. Stu, Eloise, Claire, and Danny, I love you with all my heart and am so grateful for the wonderful life we share. Thank you for supporting my dreams and helping me to fulfil them.

Contents

Part Two: The Interactions

Note to the Reader

This book is a true account of my paranormal encounters. It also includes the experiences of others as told to me by family members, friends, and patients. Due to the personal nature of the stories, some names and identifying features have been changed in order to preserve the privacy of those involved.

Although the events described are factual, in some instances time frames have been condensed for narrative purposes.

—Barbara Parks

I shall not commit the fashionable stupidity of regarding everything I cannot explain as a fraud.

—CARL JUNG

Introduction

It wasn't so very long ago that the spirit world terrified me and I rejected anything connected to ghosts and the paranormal. This was due to my experiences as a teenager, whereby I was subjected to a five-year spate of poltergeist activity that began when I was thirteen.

I felt powerless and lived through my adolescence in a state of perpetual terror. Little did I know that my fear was fuelling the paranormal events. Teamed with my awakening clairvoyance, it provided a formidable power source that allowed the poltergeist to take hold.

In my late twenties I began to realise that my encounters with ghosts were not random strokes of bad luck but were the result of my clairvoyance. It occurred to me that rather than being a victim, I was in fact extremely fortunate to be blessed with a sensitivity that few people possess.

Working through my fears has not been easy, but it is a journey I would willingly undertake again. I have emerged strong and enlightened, and grateful for my glimpses of the immeasurable potential of the human soul.

My experiences have shown me that we are so very much more than our material existence suggests. Death is not the impenetrable barrier we sometimes imagine it to be. The physical mantle we carry through life is little more than a shell, and when we shed it at the end of our earthly lives, we are no less real or potent.

Coming to this realisation has been a blessing. It has made me view life with positivity and joy. I hope that by reading this book others will glean a similar sense of joyousness as they are reminded of their true spirit selves and come to understand that death is by no means the end of our journey.

Part One

The Journey

Chapter One

The Beginning

My story begins in Sydney, Australia, in 1969, as I entered the world in the convent-run austerity of Camperdown Hospital. It is suggested that those who have experienced a brush with death often possess paranormal abilities, and I have often wondered whether my precarious start to life may account for my clairvoyance.

My parents emigrated from Croatia in 1967, with little more than a suitcase each and my two siblings in tow. My brother Luka was born the following year, by which time they had left the Bonegilla migrant camp and were renting a small terrace house in Camperdown. By the time Luka was five months old, I was already on the way.

Seven months into her pregnancy, my mother was crippled by severely infected ingrown toenails. She was referred to a specialist on Macquarie Street, a prestigious stretch of

Circa 1955: My parents, high school sweethearts aged 15 and 17.

medical practices in the heart of Sydney. The surgeon was brash and unsympathetic, and his impatience at my mother's broken English was obvious. After a cursory glance at her toes, he scheduled surgery for the following day. He failed to take my mother's medical history or even conduct a physical examination. He was oblivious to the fact that my mother was thirty-four weeks pregnant, presuming her to be grossly overweight.

He therefore had no qualms about performing the surgery under general anaesthetic, little suspecting he was placing an unborn child's life at risk. It was not until my premature delivery two weeks later that anyone realised something was wrong.

I was born jaundiced and unresponsive; the nuns who delivered me could not hide their alarm at my appearance.

From the sagging skin that hung off me like that of an old woman, it was obvious that I had lost weight in utero, and it is believed that I had been in foetal distress for the fortnight since my mother's surgery. My parents were warned that I might not survive.

Barely breathing, I was immediately rushed to the neonatal unit. One of the nuns took me in her arms and ran down the drafty corridor, where she was intercepted by my father. Horrified that I was still damp and naked, he instantly lost confidence in the standard of care and insisted on taking me home.

Despite the nun's attempts to convince him that I stood the greatest chance of survival in the special care unit, my father refused to be swayed. As soon as my vital signs were stabilised, I was bundled up and entrusted to my parents' care under the proviso that they sign a form relinquishing the hospital of any liability should I die.

I don't know if I would have been brave enough to have made a similar decision for my own children, but my father assures me he had no doubt whatsoever that he was doing the right thing. Perhaps if I had been his first child he wouldn't have been so brazen, but since I was his fourth, he had every confidence that I would be fine.

Within a couple of hours we were on our way home, with a brief stop at the chemist to buy four hot water bottles. These were to be nestled amongst my sheets and blankets, creating a cosy makeshift humidicrib.

The alarm clock was reset every two hours, at which time my parents refilled not only the hot water bottles but also my perpetually hungry belly. I was checked and rechecked, rocked and cuddled, my two oldest siblings actively involved in my round-the-clock care.

Within a couple of weeks my family's efforts began to pay off as the yellow tinge of my skin faded and my flaccid skin began to fill. My parents' pride in their fourth born was quickly crushed, however, when Karla (my mother's soon-to-be ex-best friend) dropped by to meet the new arrival.

She studied me for a moment as I lay in my cot, and then proclaimed me to be *the ugliest baby she had ever seen*. My scandalised mother wasted no time in escorting her to the door, ejecting Karla from her house and her life in one fell swoop.

Although my parents assure me that I was a beautiful baby, I can't help but think that there may have been some substance to Karla's blunt appraisal. Interestingly, there is not a single baby photo of me in existence, which makes me wonder if this is a direct result of my less than pleasant looks!

My earliest memories stretch back to when I was not quite three, and invariably take place at night. They are flashbacks of the faces that floated by my bedside, overtaking the darkness like a wallpaper of black and white photographs. Their nightly appearance was comforting and as much a part of my bedtime ritual as my cup of warm milk and my frayed pink blanket, which I called Dekica.

My regimented bedtime routine became quite the family joke, as even though I was little more than a toddler, I was very set in my ways. My parents and older siblings knew I would not go to sleep without my warm milk in its pink and white sippy cup, yet when they offered it to me before bed, I would refuse it without fail.

Once I was settled into bed, however, I was ready for my nightcap. I would wait a minute or so and then begin a barely audible chant of *Milk with sugar, Miiiii-iiiiiilk!* I would steadily build in volume until I was yelling at the top of my voice: *MILK WITH SUGAR, MIIIII-IIIIIILK!!!!* The sugared milk was of course ready and waiting for me, but for the purpose of their amusement my family would allow my requests to reach a crescendo before proffering the coveted milk.

I relished lying in the darkness as I sipped the sweet milk, tickling my face with the frayed edge of Dekica whilst I watched the faces appear before me. One frequent group of visitors included a dozen or so Asian children who looked barely older than I was. I remember wondering if they were eyeing my milk, and held on to my cup tightly!

Sometimes the faces were preceded by clusters of tiny red and blue lights. They flickered near the ceiling, slowly making their way towards me until I was surrounded by their brilliance. It was as though they were announcing the arrival of the faces that would inevitably follow. I thought the lights were beautiful, and could sometimes hear them buzzing as they brushed against my face.

At first I thought little of these apparitions, as they had been part of my nightscape for as long as I could remember. It wasn't until I started school that I began to question them, wanting to know who they were and why they showed themselves to me time and time again. But the faces remained silent, so I sought the answers from my parents. When they dismissed the apparitions as a case of tired eyes playing tricks on me, I believed them, and continued to do so until well into my teens.

I also remember the sensation of floating out of my bed and looking down on my sleeping self from above. This experience was accompanied by a sense of hollowness in the pit of my stomach and pressure in the front of my skull, feelings that come back to me now as I recall them. These episodes were involuntary, unpredictable, and extremely frightening.

The most vivid of my floating memories happened just before my fourth birthday, and began like any of the countless others that had preceded it. One minute I was tucked up in bed drifting off to sleep, and the next I was wedged up near the cornice, overwhelmed by a sense of helplessness and the feeling that this was somehow *wrong*. The familiar sick sensation began to wash over me as I looked down at the room beneath me, longing to be back in my bed below.

My wish came to fruition sooner than I expected, so forcefully and abruptly that I wondered if I would've been better off had I maintained my quiet vantage point.

A thunderous voice echoed through my bedroom, cutting through the silence with unmistakable menace.

"YOU WILL DIE!"

I slammed into my bed with violent force, my head thudding and my heart racing. It was then that I began to scream. My sister, Vlasta, rushed over to my bed and tried to comfort me, but I couldn't be consoled.

"God said I'm going to die!" I sobbed hysterically.

Circa 1972: (L–R) Me, Luka, Duro, and Vlasta (standing).
This was around the time of the "You will die!" episode.

Vlasta summoned our parents, who rushed in with assurances that of course I had been dreaming. They reminded me that God loved me and would never want to frighten me.

"He did!" I insisted. "He shouted at me!"

After much consternation I eventually accepted that the angry voice could have belonged to someone other than God, but I refused to believe that I was dreaming, mostly because I knew that I had floated out of my bed so many times before.

Thankfully this was the last time I floated out of my body. Perhaps my fears were beginning to anchor me and cloud my spiritual sensitivities. It was the first time that the spirit world had frightened me, and as a result I began to close myself off.

It is only looking back now that I realise these experiences heralded the arrival of the visitors from the other side. My spiritual journey has since followed a tortuous path. My early acceptance of the spirit world was replaced by terror in my teens, when I was subjected to disturbing physical phenomena. I have been thrown from ladders and bombarded with flying objects. Cabinets have flung open before me, their contents thrown in my face. Despite happening over twenty years ago, the memories are vivid and still make me shudder.

The more I tried to shut out the spirits, the more desperate they became for acknowledgement. Consequently, their attention-seeking behaviour escalated to what I suspect was frustration-fuelled rage.

Now that I am in my forties and have acknowledged my clairvoyant abilities, the spirits have stopped screaming for my attention. I have accepted that spirits walk among us, and that they are nowhere near as frightening as I had once thought.

Chapter Two

Ghosts and Spirits: A Brief Overview

It's important to differentiate between ghosts and spirits, as it's common for these terms to be used interchangeably. It was many years before I realised there was a difference, so allow me to spare you the same confusion before we progress any further.

In my younger days, I considered all the entities I came in contact with to be ghosts. As time went on, I came to notice that although some of my visions absolutely terrified me, others radiated a sense of positivity and calm. I began to make the distinction between *good ghosts* and *bad ghosts.*

As my clairvoyant abilities became progressively more honed, I also noticed a difference in their appearance, which I now know is a direct reflection of a soul's progression on the spiritual ladder. The good ghosts were radiant and appeared to be glowing, whereas the bad ghosts were invariably dark and appeared much more dense. In some instances they appeared almost solid, which I have since discovered is due to their heavier vibration.

It is obvious to me now that the good ghosts are actually spirits, and are very different from the ghosts I had inadvertently grouped them with. These days I can differentiate between ghosts and spirits in an instant, and wonder how I could ever have imagined them to be one and the same!

Spirits are souls who are continuing to progress on their spiritual journey and have successfully transitioned from the material to the spirit world. They are aware of their surroundings and, given the right circumstances, are able to interact with the living. They may be souls we have known prior to incarnating, or loved ones who have passed away. Spirits are high-vibrational, evolved beings, and to the clairvoyant eye they radiate light. It is possible to capture this type of spirit energy in photographs as bright, glowing orbs, but more on this later.

My encounters with spirits are invariably uplifting, unlike my experiences with ghosts, which still have the ability to scare me.

Ghosts are believed to be deceased persons who have yet to cross over to the higher realms. Some souls become trapped in the lower astral planes, usually because they don't realise they are dead or are just unwilling to cross over. This is often the case when the death is sudden, such as a murder or an accident.

In most cases, at the point of death the person's guides will help them to advance to the higher spiritual planes, but there are some who refuse to leave the world they feel most comfortable in. There are also others who refuse to continue on their spiritual journey due to unfinished business. These are considered to be earthbound entities, as they are failing to progress on their spiritual journey.

Hauntings are a phenomenon unto themselves, of which there seem to be three distinct types. With one type of haunting, the theory is that the "ghosts" are actually energy imprints, and as such have no awareness of the people who see them. This type of ghostly sighting is believed to be a replay of emotionally charged events that transpired some time ago, thereby leaving a psychic imprint on a particular place. That is why reports of hauntings usually feature distraught-looking entities aimlessly pacing through the same geographical location time and time again, as the event continues to replay itself.

A famous example of this type of haunting is that of Treasurer's House in the English county of York. There have been numerous accounts of a legion of Roman soldiers marching through a stone wall in the cellar, complete with sounding horns and the deafening thud of marching boots and horses' hooves. Due to the heightened emotions of soldiers marching to war, the event has been energetically imprinted on the location where it first occurred, despite happening over two thousand years ago.

The second type of haunting involves a sentient being who has failed to cross over. These hauntings are often fuelled by negative emotions such as anger, fear, or sorrow, as the departed soul has failed to progress beyond a negative event that occurred during his or her lifetime. The manifestation of these ghosts is fuelled largely by human emotion, which would explain why people who are frightened or emotionally vulnerable tend to encourage the manifestation of these earthbound entities.

The third type of haunting involves poltergeists, whereby there is an actual physical disturbance within a given location or around a particular person. There are two theories with regard to poltergeists, both involving a focus person, usually a teenage girl, around which the events occur. One suggestion is that the psychic energy of the focus person is actually responsible for creating the disturbance, manifesting as unconscious telekinesis, whereby the subject is unwittingly throwing objects around with his or her unacknowledged paranormal abilities. The angst commonly associated with adolescence is thought to provide additional telekinetic energy to power the disturbance.

A variation of this hypothesis is that an earthbound entity is using the adolescent's emotional upheaval as its source of power, thereby focussing on a particular individual as it wreaks havoc within the household.

With regard to my own encounters with poltergeists, I imagine my teenage experiences to have been a combination of both these theories. Whilst my fear and untapped psychic energy may well have given rise to some of the events that occurred, I can't accept that all of my paranormal encounters were of my own creation. Had I not seen figures manifest before me, I may have believed this to be possible, but I am without a doubt that some of the frightening experiences I endured were the result of the attentions of mischievous ghosts.

Now we go back to where my nightmare began, in a nondescript house on the Kensington Avenues, which just happened to be rife with ghosts.

The House on Sixth Avenue

We moved into a 1940s house in Kensington when I was seven years old. We had spent the previous two years in South Africa, as my father's engineering expertise had caught the attention of a Johannesburg-based mining company. As

Sydney, 1973: My siblings and I with Mum on the front porch of our home in Sydney. This was the house where the Asian children's faces first appeared to me.

much as we had enjoyed our African adventure, we were all glad to be moving back home.

Instead of returning to Sydney, however, my parents opted for the quieter pace of Perth, Western Australia. The suburb of Kensington seemed like the perfect place to settle, its quiet leafy streets just a ten-minute drive from the city.

Our new home was a red brick and tile bungalow, very much like the other former housing-commission homes that lined the street. It had been empty for over a year, and when we first went to inspect it, we were overwhelmed by its mustiness and obvious neglect.

From the moment I first walked through the front door I found the house creepy, and was particularly ill at ease in the sunken lounge area. My parents assured me that new carpets and a coat of paint would make the house lovely. I was unconvinced.

Despite the house's creepiness, the first few years spent there were uneventful. I was focussed on adjusting to my fourth school in as many years, as I was once again subjected to the glaring scrutiny of being the new kid.

Compared to the school I had just left, Kensington Primary School was dated and tiny. It was little more than two bitumen quadrangles, framed by musty wooden verandas that led to its red-brick classrooms. It was built in the 1920s and had seen little change since, and on my first day I felt as though I had slipped back into an earlier time.

It was a rainy day and the smell of damp wood and raincoats filled the verandas as I was led to my new classroom by the school principal. I was introduced to the year-three teacher, Miss Llewellyn, and silence engulfed the previously raucous class as they checked out the scrawny girl standing before them. I was trembling as Miss Llewellyn put her hand on my shoulder: "Say hello to Barbara, everyone. She's moved here all the way from South Africa!"

She led me to my desk and asked me to put my few belongings inside it, after which we would "have a little chat." I mistakenly presumed this to mean she wanted to speak to me immediately, and hurriedly emptied my school bag and walked to the front of the class. As she looked at me blank-faced, I realised my error.

"Is something the matter?" she asked.

I wanted to shout "I thought you wanted to talk to me!" but was momentarily struck dumb as the entire class waited for my response. I longed for escape, and racked my brain to find a plausible explanation for why I was out of my seat.

And then, in a torrent of tears, I blurted out the best thing I could come up with. "I … I haven't got any pencils!" Miss Llewellyn put her arm around me as the classroom exploded into laughter. "That's okay," she said. "We have plenty of pencils here." She ushered me back to my desk where I sat mortified until recess, knowing it would be a long, slow recovery to redeem myself after my memorable start.

Somehow I captured the attentions of Christelle Adams, who as far as I could make out seemed to be the most popular girl in the class. I was confused by her friendship, as she continually sought out my company yet thrived on being nasty to me. She claimed we were best friends but habitually put me down. "It's a real shame about your vampire teeth," she told me. "You might be pretty if it weren't for them." Or when some boys were paying me attention, she told me they just felt sorry for me.

The Arrival

My sporadic friendship with Christelle continued for several years, despite its underlying tensions. As thirteen-year-olds, we were polar opposites in both looks and attitudes. She was dark-skinned and buxom with thick, curly hair. I was pale, wispy-haired, and flat-chested, a misfortune Christelle never failed to remark upon. Christelle was consumed with her appearance and the opposite sex; I was fixated on being top of the class. I could never quite understand what it was that linked us together, yet despite our glaring differences our friendship struggled on.

In fact it was at Christelle's house that I became reacquainted with ghosts, after a merciful reprieve of almost ten years.

Christelle lived less than one hundred meters away, in a rundown old house opposite the primary school. I sometimes made the dash around the corner to say hi, knowing I could make the round trip (and perhaps even squeeze in a quick drink) without being missed. It was on one such mission that Christelle and I sat in the lounge room of her house when we heard footsteps. No one else was at home.

"It's the ghost," Christelle said matter-of-factly, "the old guy who used to live here." The back door slammed and she barely reacted, whilst I was incredulous that she could remain so calm. I questioned whether she was playing tricks on me, but when the door opened and shut yet again, she jumped up, suddenly on edge.

I left shortly after, and suggested that Christelle come stay at my house until her parents got home. She casually accepted, but I was in no doubt that her nonchalance belied the fear hiding underneath, and I couldn't help but feel sorry for her misfortune of living with a ghost.

Little did I know that I would soon have a ghost of my own, with many more to follow.

The paranormal events at the Kensington house began insidiously, so much so that at first it was easy to dismiss them and try to convince ourselves that there was nothing sinister among us. Lights flashing on and off were thought to be electrical faults, and broken and missing items were blamed on visiting children. Yet despite the denial, there was always an underlying heaviness, the feeling that something was not quite right. It was the same heaviness that I felt at Christelle's house.

Although the paranormal activity came to the fore in 1982, other family members noticed signs of a disturbance well before this. My brother Luka recalls playing with his toys in the long sunken lounge room when he was twelve years old, two years before I experienced anything ominous myself.

Luka was sitting on the carpet as he played with a recent Christmas gift, a tall plastic crane with a telescopic jib. It had a grey metal hook that dangled from a retractable string, and Luka arranged small loads around the floor for his crane

The Kensington house, 1977: Duro and Vlasta stand behind me, Luka, and our cousin Anita. Mum lurks on the front porch in a very scary dressing gown!

to collect. He was absorbed in his game when he detected movement out of the corner of his eye and turned to see the loaded-up hook swinging gently from side to side. He watched the hook gain momentum, until it was a pendulous blur of ever-increasing size. The crane itself soon began to shift, leaning from side to side until it crashed in a heap. The whole display lasted for less than a minute, and Luka wasted no time as he bolted for the door. In what was to later become a repeated sign of its presence, the ghost slammed the door shut right before my brother's face.

When he relayed the incident to my parents, they suggested that there may have been a mild earth tremor, but their explanation offered as little comfort to my brother as it did to them.

It was some weeks later that our cousin Anita came to stay, blissfully unaware of the nascent disturbance in our home. Since nothing untoward had happened since the crane incident, we had almost forgotten about the unsettling episode ourselves.

We spent the evening watching movies in the sunken lounge room, where Anita was later settled on a fold-out bed. We finished up at around midnight, and the house fell into darkness. The night was seemingly uneventful, and it was only at breakfast the following morning that we realised something unusual had transpired. Anita was giggling as she looked towards Luka sitting across from her at the kitchen table.

"What was up with you last night?" she asked. My brother looked back at her blankly, totally at a loss as to what she was referring to. "Any reason you spent the night sitting on the stairs staring at me?"

"Oh right," said Anita. "You didn't answer me last night and you're not answering now…" She resumed eating her breakfast, resigned to the fact that her cousin was an oddball, and was happy to let the matter rest.

When I pressed her further, she told me she saw Luka sitting on the stairs several times throughout the course of the night. At one point she asked Luka what he was doing, but since he did not answer, she promptly fell back to sleep.

Luka assured us that he had by no means kept watch over his slumbering cousin, but Anita was just as adamant that he had.

It then dawned on us that the boy on the stairs had not been Luka at all, and we were shaken by the thought that the young night watchman may have been a ghost. The puzzle pieces began to fit together as we recalled the crane incident a few weeks earlier. *Was this the ghost that had knocked over Luka's crane? And why had he slammed the door in my brother's face?*

Although I was definitely frightened by the thought of a ghost in the house, I was relieved that his attention had not been directed at me. I didn't realise that there was going to be a shift in attention, and that in less than two years the focus would be me.

Chapter Three

Thirteen

Christelle's haunted house played on my mind and stirred up memories of the ghostly boy. Although the two years since had been incident-free, I couldn't help worrying if our home harboured ghosts as well.

I often felt as though someone was watching me, and I became terrified of the dark. Despite my fears, I was simultaneously drawn to and repulsed by the paranormal, and *Reader's Digest Tales of the Unexpected* was my favourite book. It was around this time that the television programme *Ripley's Believe It or Not!* went to air, and often featured tales of ghostly encounters. Against my better judgement I was a frequent viewer, and more often than not found myself sleepless for several nights as a result.

One particular evening, my parents and I watched an episode featuring the famous mystic Uri Geller, renowned for his psychic abilities and telekinetic spoon bending. I flippantly commented that when I was younger I thought I was psychic. No sooner did the words come out of my mouth than the glass in my hand splintered. A lip-shaped sliver broke off and flew into the air, shooting up towards the ceiling before landing back in my drink.

We were momentarily speechless as we tried to gauge what had just happened. I looked towards my parents, who were equally bewildered, as we searched for a plausible explanation for the self-destructing glass.

"Is somebody trying to tell me something?" I laughed nervously. My mother took the glass from my hand and went into the kitchen to wash it. She retained the lip-shaped shard, and dropped it into the broken glass. She covered the glass with cling wrap, lest the wayward sliver head skyward again. It was placed in our dresser and remained there for several years, as proof of the strangeness in our midst.

When I turned thirteen, there was a reshuffle of bedrooms and I found myself relocated to the long, narrow lounge room at the back of the house. I had felt uneasy in this room since we moved in six years earlier, but the excitement of having my own bedroom overrode my misgivings. There wasn't a proper door, just an accordion-style screen, which had memorably slammed shut in front of Luka's face two years earlier. I tried to put this out of my head, reminding myself that it was a long time ago.

Despite the presence of my bed, with its floral bedspread, the room had not shaken its lounge room ambience and had failed miserably in its transformation into a young girl's bedroom. A heavy wooden mask (a souvenir from our days in South Africa) hung over the wall light beside the bed, giving the impression that its eyes were glowing and observing my every move. Irrespective of the weather, the room always felt cold.

I shared my new bedroom with a garish shop mannequin, which stood by the window in Croatian national dress. Her priceless gown was a gift from my Auntie Barbara, and was adorned with coins and delicate gold thread. Made of white linen, it was heavily embroidered in vivid blues and reds. My parents bought the mannequin to show off the gown to its best advantage, and displayed her in the sunken lounge room, where she startled first-time guests. We christened her Maya in an attempt to make her seem less sinister, but I never managed to warm to her vacant, staring face.

Since the new lounge room was not large enough to accommodate Maya, she maintained her position in my bedroom, opposite the wooden mask. I was hard-pressed to work out which I found more creepy. It was around this time that I took to sleeping with my head under the covers, a habit I have yet to shake!

The possibility of there being a ghost among us left me feeling anxious, whereas Luka seemed to thrive on the notoriety that came with living in a haunted house. After the initial shock of the first few occurrences, Luka decided that the ghost was harmless and he no longer felt afraid. Quite the contrary, he found the whole concept exciting! Having always been a joker, he used the situation to best advantage, and couldn't resist setting up fake ghostly activity when friends came to visit.

On one such occasion my friend Jo and I were sitting in the front lounge room whilst our parents were preparing a barbecue in the backyard. Jo knew that we suspected our house was haunted and was more than a little apprehensive each time she came to visit.

I expected the worst when Luka walked in and began to tease her, asking if she'd noticed anything unusual.

"I reckon someone's here tonight," he said. "I've just got that creepy feeling that something's going to happen…"

Having set the scene, he plonked himself on the sofa opposite us and pretended to watch TV. And then, with a loud, jarring crash, the metal fire poker that sat beside the fireplace was flung from its stand and slammed into the floor several feet away. Jo's high-pitched scream was loud enough to seize our parents' attention, and even though I felt certain Luka was responsible, my heart was racing as we ran into the backyard.

Once we calmed down, I assured Jo that my brother was playing tricks on us. Despite knowing that Luka was the culprit, we decided to preserve our nerves and refused to go back into the lounge room, just in case he had rigged up any more heart-stopping displays. We sat in the backyard games room instead, comforted by the presence of our parents just beyond its glass sliding doors.

Just as we were composing ourselves, there was a deafening crash against the games room wall, and the mirror that was hanging beside us came flying off its hook. It landed on the carpet by our feet, and although it didn't break, the loud bang and the spectacle of the flying mirror sent us into a tailspin once again. We questioned how Luka could possibly have engineered such a prank, especially since he was not in the room at the time.

We had almost convinced ourselves that the poltergeist activity was genuine this time when Luka was discovered skulking in the bushes behind the games room. Feeling somewhat guilty about the resounding success of his prank, he admitted that he banged on the games room wall to scare us. The added dimension of the flying mirror was an unexpected fluke, and he confessed he did not expect his ruse to be so effective!

He also admitted to setting up the fire-poker episode in the lounge room. When we went to investigate, we discovered that on the base of the poker he'd tied some fishing line, which he proceeded to tug at an opportune moment. Jo and I were furious with him, but our relief overrode our anger and we vowed to never let him frighten us again.

In the coming months as the genuine poltergeist activity escalated, my first thought was always that Luka was somehow behind it. I was desperate to believe that there was a logical explanation for the increasingly frequent disturbances, but I knew we were dealing with something more sinister than a childish hoax. My fears snowballed and I felt progressively more vulnerable as the whole family began to realise this was no longer a joke.

A Death in Croatia

One memorable afternoon, I sat in the front yard petting the dogs, my skinny thirteen-year-old legs baking together with the brown summer lawn. Some kids a couple of houses down were braving the near-melting asphalt in a half-hearted game of cricket. The rhythmic thwacks and shuffles were interspersed with the occasional "Howzat!," but there was little energy to be mustered in the stifling summer heat. Hungry and hot, I made my way inside for lunch.

As I walked into the dark lounge room I was momentarily blinded, as my eyes struggled to adjust to the gloom. The curtains were drawn and the air conditioner pumped at full capacity. My parents and brothers stared at the TV screen before them, transfixed by the cricket match. Two large pizzas sat on the coffee table, and my family chewed distractedly without taking their eyes off the screen. Wishing to avoid the relentless drone of the television, I loaded up my plate and headed to my bedroom.

It wasn't long before the monotonous commentary of the cricket match was disrupted by the phone ringing. The wall phone hung just outside my bedroom, but I knew better than to rush to answer it. My father, being of typically strict European ilk, preferred to vet incoming phone calls. On the occasions when the unfortunate caller asked to speak to one of us kids without stating their identity first, he demanded "Who is that?" so gruffly that I was always astounded the caller didn't hang up immediately, vowing never to call again!

I was relieved to realise the call was for my father, as he broke into a torrent of loud Croatian. His initial exuberance was suddenly tempered, and after a very long silence he simply thanked whoever was on the other end of the line and returned the phone to its cradle. The cricket sounds still filtered through from the front lounge, just long enough for him to cross the house and snap the TV into silence. His Uncle Emil had died.

I barely knew my father's much-loved uncle, having met him only once whilst holidaying in Croatia, so I couldn't muster the appropriate display of grief I imagined was expected of me. I thought it best to keep a low profile and stayed in my room, until I was eventually lured out by my steadily increasing hunger. The sun had long since set by the time I ventured into the kitchen, where my brothers and sister sat in conference on the breakfast bar stools. I surveyed the bench tops and stove for signs of dinner, and was dismayed to see that they were bare. My stomach rumbled in protest, but not wishing to betray my indifference to Uncle Emil's passing, I made no comment and headed to the bathroom.

There it hit me. My apathy was replaced by an overwhelming sense of alarm and I was suddenly consumed by terror. *What if Uncle Emil's ghost comes?* By this time my fear of ghosts had well and truly established itself, and I was tuned in enough to know that they seemed to gravitate towards me.

"Please, God," I muttered under my breath. "Please don't let him come to me!" I was torn between guilt and panic, guilt for not feeling sad about Uncle Emil dying and absolute panic at the prospect he would appear to me.

I stood at the bathroom basin washing my hands. The oval mirror before me doubled as my father's shaving cabinet. I stared into the mirror, trembling as I repeated my mantra. "Please, God, don't let him come. Please, God!" And then my fears were realized and I screamed. "Pleeeeeeeease!"

The cabinet flung open of its own accord, its door narrowly missing my face as it travelled its sudden and violent arc. It briefly lay wide open, trembling on its hinges. And then worse, my father's shaving implements, including his treasured porcelain shaving mug (a gift from his deceased father some twenty years earlier), were forcibly flung from the cabinet. They flew past me and clattered onto the tiles by my feet. The shaving mug travelled noisily across the floor, where it briefly rolled back and forth before settling into silence. I couldn't stop screaming.

Paralysed by fear, my feet stayed firmly rooted to the ground. My brothers were pounding on the bathroom door, fruitlessly turning the handle; they kept banging and shouting. After a few seconds I felt my body slacken and scrambled for the door. I unlocked it with shaking hands and fell into the hallway. "It was Uncle Emil's ghost," I sobbed. "Uncle Emil's ghost came!"

By now my whole family was standing before me, blank-faced and petrified.

The following Sunday we were duly despatched to the Holy Cross Church for mass, on the surface to light candles and pray for Uncle Emil's soul, but just as pertinently (though not mentioned) to pray for protection within our household.

Our usual priest was not at the pulpit, and in his place a slight, effeminate priest stood in front of the congregation. Before I had time to censure myself, I mentally ran through a list of criticisms about my innocent target, from the sing-song way he spoke to his immaculately blow-dried hair.

The more I berated myself, the more readily the unchari-table thoughts popped into my head. Trying to suppress them only served to ignite them further. I was on a roll! I was horri-fied by my irreverence, but not enough to block the criticisms that kept popping into my head. *Nice lisp! He's soooooo girly! Bet he doesn't even have his own congregation … And worst of all … I wonder if he's gay?*

Stop! I implored myself, but the thoughts just kept com-ing. I was appalled at my inner dialogue, and felt sick at the thought of my imminent confession, which was to take place straight after the service. I spent the entire mass debating with myself. *Do I confess all the spiteful thoughts I've been hav-ing? Or do I just resign myself to burning in the fires of hell for-ever?* The service passed by in a blur, as I mumbled through the responses and mouthed the hymns in nervous anticipa-tion of what lay ahead.

All too soon it was time to confess. Still undecided, I entered the small cubicle, seated myself, and made the sign of the cross. I could just make out the priest's silhouette behind the gauzy screen between us.

"Forgive me, Father, for I have sinned … It has been four weeks since my last confession."

I waited for the invitation to divulge my transgressions, and then slowly reeled through my sins. I told him about my swearing and my frequent fights with my brother, but I did not tell the priest about the thoughts I had just been entertaining about him.

I chickened out, and justified my decision by telling myself that I could not possibly offend him with my derision. I was relieved but felt like a coward, and I was convinced that God was furious with me. From then on I imagined that I had lost God's protection, and that I was at the mercy of the ghosts. And from then on, it only got worse.

Chapter Four

Escalation

My great uncle's death marked the official acknowledgement of paranormal activity in our home. We could no longer live in denial; there was no doubt that there were ghosts in our midst.

In the year that followed, my ghostly encounters became steadily more frequent. I felt increasingly victimised, and the hollow dread that sat permanently in my stomach intensified each night as darkness fell.

The visits by the recently departed were just part of the passing parade that stood by my bedside. I was usually aware of who these spirits were, as they made one brief appearance and then disappeared to wherever souls travel on the next phase of their journey. At the very most they made an attention-seeking ruckus in a dramatic goodbye, as Uncle Emil had done. Despite my rationalisations that they had only come to say goodbye, I still found their visits frightening.

The ghost boy who had made himself known to us two years earlier also put in the occasional appearance. Although he was mischievous and could easily scare us, his presence was reasonably benign.

It was the dark, shadowy figures that scared me the most. They seemed to linger at the periphery of my vision, creating an uneasiness that steadily pervaded our home.

There was one particular entity I came to think of as *the dark man,* although I felt him more than I could see him. His increasingly frequent visits were identifiable by the preceding thickness of the air, the atmosphere becoming so heavy it felt as though I could slice through it with a machete. We first became aware of him on a cold winter's evening in 1982, just as we sat down to dinner.

As is the custom, a flagon of homemade red wine sat in the middle of the table. There was a large pot of sarma (cabbage leaves stuffed with a mixture of pork and rice) and chunks of rustic homemade bread. My mother had just finished dishing up when we first noticed his presence. It began with a small rasping sound, a scrape of metal on glass that was barely audible. It was soon obvious where the sound was coming from, and we looked towards the flagon of wine before us. Its metal lid twisted and shot off, flinging upwards with enough force to hit the ceiling. It fell back, landing gently on the bottle, where it remained quietly in repose as though nothing had happened.

I felt the urge to run, but remained firmly rooted to my chair. I looked around at my family members, who, except for my parents, stared back at me, stunned. My father was examining the bottle cap, picking up the flagon, sniffing its contents. My mother had resumed eating as though nothing had happened. My brother Luka was the first to break the silence. "What the hell was that?"

"It's the gases," my father said distractedly. "Alcoholic gases; they build up in the bottle..." With that he poured wine for us all. As is the Croatian tradition, he poured a small measure into the children's glasses as well. He topped them up with water until the glass held a subtle pink blush, its vinegary sourness accompanying most evening meals.

We resumed our dinner. I desperately wanted to believe my father's explanation for the wayward flagon, but it was obvious that we were dealing with something more sinister than an accumulation of gases. There was little time to doubt, as we were barely halfway through the meal when chaos broke out in the next room.

It began with an ear splitting bang as the laundry cupboard was flung open. We heard a deafening crash followed by glass shattering. The whole room began to shake; it felt as though we were in the midst of an earthquake. Although the bedlam lasted for just a few seconds, it felt never-ending. Dad rushed into the laundry as soon as the noises began and stood in the doorway, frozen by the scene before him. The rest of us cowered behind him; my eyes were squeezed tightly shut and my hands were clamped over my ears.

We didn't advance until it was over, and then quietly, one by one, we walked into the laundry. Open-mouthed, we surveyed the damage. The greying linoleum was strewn with broken glass and the splintered broken frames of our family photos. The photos themselves lay crumpled in the midst of the debris, our own idiot faces grinning at us from the chaos. Wordlessly, the six of us began to clean up the wreckage, salvaging what we could and sweeping up the glass. My mother returned the damaged photographs to the top shelf of the cupboard, closing the cupboard doors firmly behind them. The family returned to the dinner table, although no one had any inclination to resume eating. I was the last one left in the laundry, crouching on the floor with a dustpan and brush, sweeping up the last of the broken glass. Suddenly there was a loud crash and I began screaming. The cupboard doors had flung open once again, the damaged photos thrown onto the floor. They had narrowly missed my head. I couldn't stop shaking. I was sobbing, inconsolable.

This was our introduction to the dark man, the shadowy figure who went on to haunt us for the next five years. Some nights it was little more than a glimpse of a fleeting black figure; at other times he announced himself with increasingly violent displays of aggression.

As time went on, it was obvious that the common denominator of these events was me. Nothing paranormal happened unless I was in the house. We also came to notice that the disturbances were generally linked to my mood at the time. If I was in a positive frame of mind, it was unlikely anything untoward would happen. But if I was anxious or

frightened, my emotions acted like a beacon, attracting negative energies and the likely manifestation of a figure at the
end of my bed.

Knowing that negativity and angst seemed to fuel the
haunting, I tried to temper my moods as much as possible.
I tried to remain positive and calm. But being a hormonal
thirteen-year-old, this was easier said than done.

The attentions of the dark man were a classic case of poltergeist activity. Poltergeists commonly focus their attention
on adolescents, feeding off emotional energy as their power
source. Teenage girls seem to be more of a target than boys,
perhaps because they are generally more emotive and are
thus less likely to suppress their anxiety and fear.

I imagine that, to a poltergeist, I would've been a particularly attractive target. My budding clairvoyance coupled with
my intense fear would've proved an irresistible combination,
as I unwittingly stoked the power source of the ghost that
was terrorising me.

Uncle Ernie

In the midst of my turmoil, I found an unexpected source
of comfort in our next-door neighbours, Gloria and Ernie.
Well into their sixties, they were longtime residents of Sixth
Avenue, having moved into their three-bedroom bungalow as
newlyweds in the 1940s.

Over the years we grew very close to our elderly neighbours. As I was only seven years old when we first moved to

A family dinner with our beloved next-door neighbours.
Ernie is at the extreme left of the photo, and Gloria is
beside him. Their daughter, Margaret, is seated farther
along the table with her family. I am seated opposite Gloria.
It was after one such dinner that Ernie suffered a massive
heart attack and died. The doorway behind Gloria leads to
the sunken lounge room, which later became my bedroom
(and the focal point of the five-year haunting). The door at
the end of the table leads to my bedroom at the time, where
Ernie's ghost would appear to me a few weeks later.

Kensington, they were a comforting constant in my day-to-day life. Dashing next door was a welcome escape.

Despite his gruff exterior, Ernie had a well-hidden gentle side, and was forever proffering jelly beans my way when he thought no one was looking. He was a typical Aussie bloke, weather-beaten and grumpy, but somehow he insinuated himself into my heart.

Gloria was grandmotherly and gorgeous, and impossible not to love. I gravitated towards her since both my grandmothers lived in Croatia, and she welcomed my regular after-school visits with open arms.

The ritual was always the same. I took their fat white Labrador, Lutzi, for a walk, and then Gloria and I sat on the low brick wall and gossiped. We watched Lutzi as she threw herself onto the lawn with increasing fervour, desperately trying to scratch her back on the sharp blades of grass. Gloria wanted to hear all about my day, and never seemed to tire of me raving about my favourite band or latest crush. When I told her about the ghosts, she didn't dismiss them. She listened intently, thoughtfully nodding her head.

"You'll be right, love," she'd say with a comforting smile.

In typically Croatian tradition, my mother's evening meals were generous enough to feed twice as many. As a result, I seemed to be forever ferrying dishes laden with food next door, the fruits of my mother's over-catering always eagerly received. Over the years Gloria and Ernie became acquainted with a dazzling array of Croatian cuisine, as they were also frequent dinner guests.

When Ernie turned sixty-six, he told me he was worried that *his number might be up.*

"W…Why would you think that?" I asked. "It's nothing serious, is it?"

"Nah," he laughed. "Nothing like that. I'm just worried that when God checks my age from up there, it'll look like ninety-nine instead of sixty-six!"

We laughed together, but my relief was superficial. I couldn't help feeling that something was wrong.

A few weeks later Gloria and Ernie joined us for a family dinner. It was a pleasantly raucous evening, and Ernie regaled us with anecdotes of his life as a steward at the local trotting club.

At the end of the evening my mother asked me to accompany Gloria and Ernie home by torchlight, as she was worried they could stumble and hurt themselves on their poorly lit driveway. Being scared of the dark, I was not overly happy about the arrangement, but allowed them to take an elbow each as we followed the dim torch beam. What should have been a two-minute walk stretched into a ten-minute ordeal as the feeble couple shuffled nervously through the darkness.

Once they were safely at their front door, I turned to bolt the fifty or so meters home. I reached the top of their driveway and froze. "Uncle Ernie!" I called out. "You still there?"

"Yes, love," he replied. "What is it?"

I don't know why, but I ran back down the driveway and kissed him. "Good night!" It was the first and last time I kissed him, as sometime after midnight he suffered a massive, fatal heart attack.

As always when somebody died, I was a bundle of nervous expectation. Even if the deceased person was only remotely connected to me (such as the friend of a friend), they still somehow gravitated towards me and invariably made their presence known. Thankfully these visits were not as dramatic as Uncle Emil's spectacular farewell a year earlier, but were compelling enough for me to anticipate some kind of contact whenever someone died.

So I wasn't in the least surprised when Uncle Ernie dropped by for his final farewell, just a week after his passing. Terrified by all means, but not at all surprised!

I had been putting off going to bed until I was absolutely exhausted, hoping I'd fall asleep straight away. On this particular evening it was almost one in the morning by the time I turned off the TV and went to bed.

As was my usual practice, I pulled the covers over my head and waited for elusive sleep. It wasn't long before I heard a low buzzing sound. The air around me felt thick and oppressive, and the panic began to rise. The buzzing became more intense, and I was surrounded by dense vibration. Although I was terrified, I had no choice but to look. I raised the covers just a fraction and peered through the darkness towards the end of my bed.

And there he was. A wavering, contorting figure, struggling to keep his form. He was pale grey and craggy, and although he didn't look like Uncle Ernie, I had no doubt that it was him. His features were sinuous and constantly changing: eyes, nose, and mouth swapping positions and in perpetual motion on his ever-twisting face. I felt as though he was sucking up my energy. I stared frozen and transfixed. I told myself it was just Uncle Ernie and there was no need to be scared, but logic and reasoning didn't stand a chance and I succumbed to feeling terrified.

Almost inaudibly, I heard a low voice penetrate the buzzing in the room. "The organ. Tell her to keep the organ!" With those words, I had no doubt it was him. Uncle Ernie's Hammond organ was his pride and joy, purchased for a whopping five thousand dollars, a fortune in the early 1980s. He was so besotted with his organ that his CB radio calling card was "Organ Grinder," as a salute to his prized possession.

Once the message was delivered, he vanished and the room resumed its normality. I ran to my parents' bedroom and told them about Uncle Ernie. My father wasn't surprised, telling me he saw a figure dart down the length of the dining room and into my bedroom a few nights earlier. Not wanting to frighten me, he kept the sighting to himself. At that time the fold-out bed sat permanently in the corner of my parents' bedroom, and I found myself more and more frequently needing to seek out its refuge.

After a restless night's sleep, I sat at the breakfast bar eating toast when my mother walked into the kitchen. By now she had stopped making excuses for the paranormal events that seemed to frequent our home, and was in no doubt that Uncle Ernie had dropped by the night before.

"You know you have to go next door and see Gloria," she said. "You should tell her what Ernie said." She poured herself a coffee and leaned back against the bench.

"Mum! No way! I can't tell her. What if I upset her?"

"You have to. Ernie came to see you for a reason; you have to pass on the message."

I was poised to argue, but knew there was no point.

"Go after breakfast," she said, and there was no further discussion.

Soon after I was ringing Gloria's front doorbell, and as soon as she heard it, Lutzi came thundering through the house.

"Lutzi!" Gloria shouted. "Lutzi, no!" Lutzi crashed against the security door in a desperate scramble to reach me, convinced I'd come to take her for a walk.

I squeezed through the partially opened door, and all eighty quivering kilos of Lutzi butted up against me. She was frantic with excitement, and Gloria had to drag her out the back door before we could even contemplate attempting a conversation.

"So how are you getting on?" I asked quietly. Gloria looked on the brink of tears but told me she was doing fine, despite missing Ernie. I took a deep breath, and before I had time to back out, I told her.

"I saw him," I said. "Last night. Uncle Ernie…"

Her eyes lit up and I was momentarily dazzled by the transformation in her face.

"Really? So did Margaret, right here in the kitchen!"

She told me that after her late waitressing shift, her daughter, Margaret, called by for a coffee and saw her father standing beside the kitchen table. Although Ernie's visit was over in a matter of seconds, both Margaret and Gloria were comforted by the thought that he was still around.

Since no message had been delivered, Gloria assumed her husband was simply dropping in to say goodbye.

Seeing this revelation as my green light, I went on to tell her about the organ and that Ernie didn't want her to sell it.

"Oh struth!" she said. "I've already put the ad in the paper." She was thoughtful for a moment, but then clasped her hands as she got up to make us some tea. "But if the old

Organ Grinder wants me to hang on to the wretched thing, then I will!"

And there in the corner, covered by a white sheet, "the wretched thing" sat for another six years until Gloria herself passed away. Never to play another note, it sat there silently in accordance with Ernie's wishes.

Rehearsal Night

When stories about my ghostly encounters began to filter through the school, I was suddenly transformed from girly swat to gothic weirdo. My schoolmates were divided in their opinions regarding the much-lauded haunting. Some were dubious and dismissive, whilst others gravitated towards me, hungry for as much detail as possible.

It's funny how the combination of daylight and being surrounded by friends instilled me with such a strong sense of false bravado. I would readily relay my most recent run-ins with ghosts, valiantly recounting each episode in minute detail. Uncle Ernie even seemed to assume some kind of posthumous celebrity status, and my friends frequently asked whether he had been around lately. His name came up so frequently that I sometimes worried whether he might not appreciate his unjustifiably ominous reputation!

Whenever some new ghost-related event occurred, I would waste no time in telling my friends. They, of course, would then tell others, until the story took on a life of its own and spread throughout the school. As much as it helped to talk to my friends about what was happening to me, my bravado invariably took a nosedive as soon as I went home.

By year twelve it was an accepted fact that I lived in a haunted house, and my friends were torn between being fascinated or scared. When the opening night of the school play was looming (ironically titled *There's No Such Thing as Ghosts*), one of my fellow castmates suggested that we schedule an extra rehearsal out of school hours. Of course it was decided that it should be held at my house, to try to *take advantage of the vibes*.

And so it was set for the following Friday; Dean and our fellow castmates would come over so we could practice our lines together.

Dean was the first to arrive at six o'clock, and Kim and Christelle arrived together shortly after. The rest of the family had gone out for the evening, so we had the house to ourselves. I didn't expect that we'd get much rehearsing done but was looking forward to catching up with my friends and having a break from study.

We started off enthusiastically and managed to run through a couple of scenes before talk inevitably turned to ghosts.

"So do you reckon Uncle Ernie's here?" asked Dean. And with as little provocation as that, there was a loud bang from the kitchen. "Your folks left yet?" he asked, trying not to betray his nervousness in front of three girls.

"Yeah, they left when you came," I replied, edging closer towards my friends.

Best buddies: Thirty years after first meeting as twelve-year-olds, Dean and I are still the closest of friends.

Bang! Again from the kitchen, only this time louder.

"There's gotta be someone in here, guys," whispered Dean. "I reckon someone's broken in because there are no cars out front...they probably think no one's home."

Our night was suddenly transformed from a bit of fun with friends to something much more sinister.

"Follow me!" he whispered.

We trailed out of my bedroom as quietly as possible, up the two steps and across the long dining room towards the kitchen. Dean turned the door handle as carefully as he could and then quickly snapped on the light. No one was there. We all bundled into the kitchen, hanging on to Dean as he led us towards the knife block, where he grabbed the largest knife. We filed towards the bathroom, where we could hear shuffling, rummaging sounds. And then, the toilet flushed and we were absolutely terrified.

"Shit!" said Dean. "A burglar wouldn't flush the toilet!"

It took every ounce of our combined courage to eventually open the bathroom door. And of course when we did, no one was there. "I suppose I won't be needing this then," said Dean as he dropped the knife to his side.

Needless to say, there was no further rehearsing that night, and we sat huddled in my bedroom, waiting for my parents to come home.

It was only a week or two later when Dean had an experience of his own, at home in his bedroom. Not wanting to scare me, he didn't tell me about it until at least a year after the event. Ever since the night of the play rehearsal, he had felt as though Uncle Ernie had followed him home. I told him later it was more likely to have been the dark man, because Uncle Ernie could not possibly have been so menacing.

Dean told me he was lying in bed one night when he suddenly saw a blanket of tiny dots overtaking the darkness. The air in the room felt thick and stifling, and his mouth began to feel dry. His body felt heavy and immovable.

All of a sudden his bedroom door swung open with a resounding crash, his heart began to race, and he found he couldn't swallow. Feeling as though he was choking, he looked towards the end of his bed and saw a large black figure looming over him, radiating a sense of evil. As is common in these encounters, Dean was frozen and unable to speak; he was at the mercy of the dark entity.

In desperation he started to speak to it in his head, hoping the message would get through and put an end to the terrifying visitation.

"Whatever I did to piss you off, I'm sorry! Please... go away!"

Almost instantly, the figure disappeared and Dean's voice and mobility were restored. The first thing he did was turn on the light, to reassure himself that the ghost had gone and everything was okay. He had a fitful night's sleep and gratefully welcomed the first light of the morning, but he was deeply shaken and it was some months before he felt safe again.

For obvious reasons, no further rehearsals were held at the house on Sixth Avenue. Sometimes I wonder if the play's title may have riled up the resident spirits. Would there have been such dramatic repercussions if we'd been rehearsing something a little less provocative? *The Sound of Music,* perhaps? I will never know for sure, but I suspect that regardless of what the play was, the poltergeist was fuelled by our fear and was ready for action.

Chapter Five

When Enough
Is Enough

Year twelve of high school was hard enough without having to contend with poltergeists. With my heart set on studying medicine, I was a committed student and rare was the night I didn't study.

My parents had a prefabricated game room built in our backyard in the early 1980s, and once the novelty of the pool table wore off, we converted the space into a communal study. By this time my older brother and sister had moved out of home, so it was just Luka and I who convened there each night. It was a fair distance from the house and was a quiet refuge from the distractions of the household.

The intensity of study temporarily dulled my sensitivity to the paranormal, particularly when I studied until very late and fell into bed exhausted. There seemed to be a lull in poltergeist activity midway through 1986, my final year of high school.

Perhaps I'd just been lulled into a false sense of security, as every once in a while my parents would call on our parish priest and arrange to have our house blessed. I really wanted to believe that the periodic sprinkling of holy water had at last taken hold, and that we had finally shaken the negativity that had permeated our house for so long.

But just as I began to feel as though the dark days were behind me, the ghosts started to fire up again.

The reprieve had been short-lived, lasting no more than a couple of months. My experience has shown me that the manifestation of ghosts is often fuelled by extremes of human emotion. As such, the tense build-up to the tertiary entrance exams provided the perfect environment for the resurgence of ghostly activity in our home.

One afternoon I conceded to my mother's requests to clean my bedroom window. I climbed the three rungs of the stepladder, teetering on the uppermost step as I tucked up the lace curtains. Once I was ready to start cleaning, I dipped the squidgy into the bucket beside me and began to sweep the suds across the glass. I had barely begun when I was shoved in the elbow, sending my hand flying across the window. I lost my balance and tumbled off the ladder. Furious, I spun around to confront Luka, convinced that he was the culprit. My anger turned to terror when I saw that no one was there. And my heart sunk as I realised it was all starting up again. I ran out of my bedroom in tears. And as confirmation that the ghosts had returned, my bedroom door slammed shut forcefully behind me.

Having long since established that intense emotion (particularly fear) seems to intensify paranormal activity, I have no idea how I could have been foolish enough to agree to watch *The Exorcist*. By now exams had finished, and my brother and I often spent the stifling summer nights in the air-conditioned refuge of my bedroom, watching movies with our friends.

Although I initially resisted the suggestion to watch the Academy Award–winning horror flick of 1973, with a little convincing I reluctantly agreed. As soon as it began, my inner voice was raging at me. *Turn the bloody thing off! Don't watch it!* But with the cavalier attitude of teenagers en masse, we sat through what has often been called the scariest movie of all time. I was gripped by fear and revulsion for its entire two-hour duration, yet stupidly I sat frozen, enduring Regan's miseries with more than a little empathy.

By the time I went to bed I was terrified and prayed feverishly to the God I hoped hadn't abandoned me. I pulled the covers over my head, leaving just a small breathing hole; I was waiting for the visit I had no doubt would come.

It began with a flicker of lights in the hallway outside my bedroom, a rapid on/off flick of the light switch, a subtle disturbance of energy. Then footsteps, the two thuds of descent down the stairs followed by the steady rhythmic footfalls of someone crossing the room. Each second stretched into a painful forever and I strained to move. My arm was paralysed and refused to inch toward the lamp switch mere centimetres away. The bedsprings squeaked and in one swift motion my chest was crushed by a dead weight on top of me. I struggled to breathe. I felt as though my life was being drawn out of me. I was powerless, immobilised and suffocating.

Breathe! I told myself, but my feeble intake of breath was enough to make me retch, as the sickening stench of decay seeped into my lungs. I felt evil encompass the room.

Eventually I managed a weak yelp and the spell was broken; the weight disappeared as swiftly as it had come. I groped for the lamp switch, but the light did little to dispel my terror. I bolted towards the door, a hysterical mess. As I reached for the handle, the screen shuddered and slammed shut before me, clamping onto its magnet, refusing to budge. I struggled to pull it open, and for the few seconds it remained fast, my hysteria escalated to the point where I could barely breathe. Eventually the door relented and I ran straight to my parents' bedroom. It took hours to calm me, and it was almost dawn by the time I was settled on the fold-out bed. And there I lay every night until we moved out a few weeks later, sleep still eluding me.

Suppression

The move to Gidgegannup was due largely to my parents' desire to live in the country, as they had long wanted to swap their cramped suburban lifestyle for some acreage. Gidgegannup lies in the hills east of the Perth metropolitan area. Despite being just twenty-five miles from the city, it's a rural retreat boasting large properties, lush rolling hills, and a generous population of kangaroos. It was the antithesis of the cramped suburban lifestyle we had just left.

Escaping the ghosts was an added advantage, although my parents didn't acknowledge the haunting as a reason for our departure. There was enough stigma attached to living in a haunted house without conceding that the ghosts had finally driven us out.

To my mind, though, my most recent encounter destroyed any chance of a long-term future in the house. I was convinced I could never feel safe there, and my parents undoubtedly knew that. After the night of *The Exorcist,* there was no way I would ever sleep in my bedroom again.

I loved our new house from the moment we moved in, mostly because it couldn't have been more different from the house we had just left. It was a bright and airy Australiana-style homestead, and was nestled between lush green paddocks on either side of its long gravel driveway. Best of all, it was only five years old and unlikely to have ghosts.

I didn't even balk at the hour-long drive to university, considering it a minor trade-off for peace of mind and a good night's sleep. The University of Western Australia (UWA) has a reputation as one of Australia's premier universities. Just a short drive from the city of Perth, it is situated on the banks of the Swan River in the suburb of Crawley.

Although I never totally shook off my anxiety, the heaviness and oppression that plagued me in Kensington seemed to lift. I felt sure that now that we had left the so-called haunted house, I could put the frightening episode behind me and embrace my new life in the country. I had, however, become extremely guarded, and rejected anything to do with the other side. No more ghost stories and no more horror movies for me. I refused to take the risk of starting it all up again. I immersed myself in my studies and embraced the hectic social life that university invariably brings.

Although there were no ghosts in the Gidgegannup house, from time to time I still saw the red and blue lights and the Asian children's faces. The sequence of their appearance was the same as when I was younger. First the red and blue lights would come flickering from a far corner of the room, and then gradually the lights would be replaced by the faces.

The faces were always the same, and there were literally dozens of them. The vision reminded me of a black and white school photograph, although sometimes the faces became animated, as if someone had released the pause button on a remote control. They would then smile and giggle and weren't threatening in the slightest; in fact they always left a sense of happiness in their wake.

Ridiculously I still believed the explanation my parents gave me when I was four. I still considered the visions to be a symptom of tiredness, and entirely believed that my eyes were just playing tricks on me. Never for a moment did I suspect that they were the product of latent clairvoyance.

Besides, I was too preoccupied to dwell on them. My new life as a university student was a hectic mix of commuting, parties, and study, with little time left for anything else.

I met a vast array of people at UWA, including a trio of grammar school boys who became part of my close circle of friends. I initially noticed them in my first-year algebra unit as they relentlessly mimicked our elderly lecturer, Beryl. They reduced the surrounding rows of the lecture theatre to a mass of poorly suppressed giggles, and I was drawn as much to their tomfoolery as their roguish good looks.

They were known only by their nicknames—Johnno, Chook, and Millsy—and it was six months into our friendship when I realised I had no idea what their real names were. But even when I discovered them, it was impossible to refer to them as anything other than their nicknames. To this day I struggle to recall the names with which they were christened!

As our friendship unfolded, I told them about my recent experiences in Kensington, offering a condensed version of the horrors that had plagued me in the preceding five years. They listened quietly, but offered little feedback. I was left wondering whether they doubted the authenticity of my stories, and I felt decidedly unsettled by their deadpan response. I found the exchange odd and it gnawed at me, so a week or so later I sought out Chook, hoping to get to the bottom of the group's unexpected reaction.

As soon as I mentioned the haunting, Chook seemed to know what was coming. He agreed that I didn't imagine the strange vibe during our previous discussion, but assured me it had nothing to do with me. Our conversation had just stirred up memories they would've preferred to forget.

Chook told me that a little over a year before, he and his mates decided to have a spur-of-the-moment séance, which they held in a caravan in his parents' backyard. They made up a crude Ouija board, in the middle of which they placed an upturned glass.

They lit a solitary gas lamp and squeezed themselves around the small fold-down table. The three of them placed a finger each on top of the glass, and half-jokingly invited any spirits present to make themselves known.

At first there was nothing, but then, almost indiscernibly, the glass began to vibrate. They felt it more than they could see it, and the buzzing sensation radiated from the tips of their fingers into the palms of their hands. Chook said that by looking at his friends' faces, he had no doubt that what was happening was real.

He told me that at first it was quite thrilling, but things started to get scary once the glass began to move.

When Johnno asked the spirit for its name, the glass started to jerk around frenetically, pointing out a jumble of meaningless letters.

Chook described the atmosphere in the caravan as suddenly shifting, and despite it being a warm summer's evening, the temperature began to plummet. Then, before they had time to abandon proceedings, the spirit took charge and terminated the séance itself.

Johnno's chair was forcibly flung backwards. It slammed into the lined metal wall of the caravan, where it teetered on its two hind legs, and in two seconds flat he was scrambling for the door.

As the three teenagers almost fell over each other in the rush to get out of the caravan, the gas lamp went out and pitched the caravan into darkness. And then as final confirmation that proceedings were over, the glass on the table shattered, spraying the terrified trio with a smattering of broken glass.

Despite these events happening more than a year prior to Chook relaying the story, the fear in his eyes was unmistakeable. It was now apparent why my Kensington stories elicited such a guarded reaction, and Chook told me he still felt nervous when he recalled the events of that night.

I was beginning to think that my ghostly encounters weren't as unique as I had thought they were, and the realisation dawned on me with conflicting emotions. It was comforting to know that I was not alone in my experiences, but it also terrified me to think that ghosts and hauntings were more prolific than I had imagined. It struck me that it was highly likely that I would run into more ghosts in the future, and the very thought of it filled me with dread.

When I recounted Chook's story to my old schoolfriend Dean, he relayed a similar experience that had occurred at his parents' holiday house a few months earlier. Dean told me about an impromptu séance he and three friends conducted, once again initiating contact via a homemade Ouija board.

The four teenagers had spent the early part of the evening drinking, and when talk turned to spirits, it wasn't long before they came up with the idea of having a séance. The Ouija board was assembled and candles lit, as the foursome sat around a small table and summoned the spirits.

Almost immediately the glass began to move, and the teenagers' questions were met with a series of rapid yes/no answers. Their excitement mounting, they wanted more, and asked the spirit to tell them its name. The glass slowed down to a steady, deliberate drag and systematically spelled out S-A-T-I-N.

Either as a result of their poor spelling skills or the alcohol they had consumed earlier, the teenagers were convinced they were communicating with the devil, and were of course terrified. They put a hasty end to proceedings, and consoled themselves with a bracing late-night drink.

When Dean relayed the story, I wondered if the séance was a ruse, and if one of his friends may have been subtly moving the glass. But given my recent history, I couldn't entirely dismiss the possibility that they were indeed communing with a ghost, either a mischievous one intent on terrifying them by impersonating Satan or one who simply had a predilection for fine fabrics! Either way the end result was the same, as the youngsters were meddling with the unknown and were left feeling vulnerable and afraid.

Since I hadn't long fled the scene of the Kensington haunting, the idea of actually initiating contact with ghosts was inconceivable to me. I couldn't comprehend why anyone would willingly summon ghosts into their lives, thereby possibly embarking on the same kind of nightmare from which I'd recently escaped.

My friends' stories stirred up my fears and strengthened my resolve to close myself off from the spirit world forever.

My good friend Deni, on one of his frequent trips to my Maylands apartment. This time he's wearing a red T-shirt instead of the red underpants!

Crossing Paths

It was around this time that I met Deni, who soon became one of my closest friends. I was seventeen years old and we were both studying science at UWA. Deni was eighteen, repeating his first year as a result of too much partying and too little studying.

We struck up a friendship immediately. Like me, Deni was Croatian, and he shared his February 2 birthday with my mother. Due to our shared heritage, we rechristened each other "Denovich" and "Barbarich," a take on the ubiquitous "ich"-ending surnames that the majority of Croatians seem to share.

Since Deni's parents lived way north in Port Hedland, he was a frequent guest at our Gidgegannup dinner table. My parents were initially taken aback by his larger-than-life character, but it wasn't long before they warmed to him and plied him with enough food and wine to satiate a small village.

Our university years felt like one long party, interspersed with frantic end-of-term cramming sessions where we attempted to make up for our slackness in the preceding weeks. Deni lost heart somewhere towards the end of second year and decided a European holiday would be just the tonic to revive his fading motivation. He took off on the trip of a lifetime, occasionally calling from public telephones to make sure I knew how much fun he was having.

Whilst travelling, Deni decided to leave university, and when he returned home he started work as a labourer with his father's building company. He was still a tearaway, partying until dawn and turning up on-site bleary-eyed and exhausted. I was still at uni, and as such we lost contact as our lives led us in radically different directions.

It was over three years before I saw Deni again. By now I was a podiatrist and had moved out of home. I had heard through mutual friends that Deni had also moved, and promised myself I would track him down and reestablish our friendship. I missed him and often berated myself for losing touch. I was swamped by the distractions of a new job and my newfound freedom.

On a mild autumn day in 1994, I moved into the first flat of my own, after sharing with my friend Claudia during my first six months of freedom. It was a small one-bedroom apartment in a complex of eight, four storeys high with two flats on each floor. Despite its pokiness, I was thrilled to have my own place; it was neat and secure, and only a stone's throw from the Swan River. Despite the backbreaking effort of lugging countless loads of my belongings up the stairs, my excitement didn't dwindle.

My reverie was broken by a familiar voice and I almost dropped the vacuum cleaner I was carrying.

"Barbarich!"

And there he was, Deni on the balcony directly below my apartment, resplendent in a pair of red underpants. "Denovich!" I called back, and soon he was bolting up the stairs and enveloping me in a bear hug. "What are you doing here?" I asked, laughing.

"I live here!" he said. And so began the closest years of our friendship. We were neighbours and best friends, supporting each other through the dramas and tribulations that early adulthood inevitably holds.

Chapter Six

Living Alone

Given my history of ghostly encounters, living alone was always going to be a challenge. Although the six years since we left Kensington had been incident-free, I just couldn't shake my deeply rooted fears. I was half-expecting a resurgence at any time.

The transition from living with Claudia to moving into an apartment of my own was made a little easier by the fact that I was surrounded by friends. Deni lived downstairs, and my next-door neighbour Karen and I soon became close. There was also a forty-something bachelor named Pete who lived on the fourth floor, who insisted on keeping a protective eye on the single ladies in the building (although looking back now I wonder if it was more of a lecherous eye than a protective one!).

Pete also assumed the self-appointed role of parking nazi, and was continually peering out his upstairs window or pacing through the car park, keeping an ever-watchful eye out for parking infringements. He was armed with a notebook and left anonymous warnings with anyone who was not parked in an appropriate bay. Pete was a portly, bearded computer geek, yet despite his quirks he was a comforting presence.

A few months after moving into my small rental, a two-bedroom apartment came up for sale in the same complex. My parents had come by for lunch on a Saturday afternoon when we noticed a "Home Open" sign directed towards the apartment directly above me. Being newly graduated, I hadn't yet considered buying a home of my own; so when my parents suggested we take a look, I was only mildly interested.

We headed upstairs and introduced ourselves to the gushing real-estate agent, who eagerly took us on a tour. Although the apartment was dated and in need of renovation, its potential was hard to ignore. To the barely contained delight of the agent, I decided to make an offer.

I was swept up in a whirlwind, as my offer was quickly accepted and financing was arranged. Before I knew it I had my first mortgage looming! I had been catapulted into the adult world of employment and responsibility in the space of a few short months, and was exhilarated as I rode the wave of my growing independence.

I called my brother Luka, who was by now an up-and-coming barrister with his own law firm in South Perth, and asked him to oversee the property settlement for me.

"I'm flat out at the moment," he said. "I'll get Stuie Parks to do it for you."

"Who's he?" I asked, feeling a little fobbed off. "Can't you just do it?"

"He's a consultant at the firm. Trust me, you'll like him."

A week later I was preparing for bed when the phone rang. I'd just finished watching *Melrose Place,* and despite it still being relatively early, I felt unwell and decided an early night was called for.

"Barbie girl!" said Luka. "I was just checking to see if you were home. I'm just down the road with Parksy."

"Actually, I was just about to go to bed. I'm not feeling too good."

"It's only nine thirty! We won't stay long. I just want to introduce you guys before he starts work on the settlement."

"But I'm already in my PJs!"

"See you in five!" he said laughing, and hung up.

I rushed into my bedroom and pulled on my jeans and a jumper. My throat was on fire and my head was beginning to throb. I resolved to get rid of my visitors as soon as possible.

There was a knock at the door just moments after I'd hurriedly dragged a comb through my hair. I opened it to see Luka grinning at me mischievously, and someone lurking in the shadows behind him.

As Stuart emerged from the darkness, I saw a face with two bruised and blackened eyes and a bent, swollen nose (which he had broken just days earlier during a game of football). He was drinking from a can of beer and was dressed in jeans and a similarly faded denim jacket. He wore a small silver earring and looked decidedly rough and ready. Despite his alarming appearance, I couldn't help feeling charmed as he handed me a small box of chocolates.

The hour-long visit distracted me from how bad I felt, but once my guests left I became all too aware of my sore throat and creeping fever. It got worse as the night progressed, as my as-yet-undiagnosed glandular fever began to take hold.

So on the most unlikely of nights, feeling far from my best, my future husband was delivered to my doorstep. As far as home delivery goes, it doesn't get any better than that!

Moving On

My budding romance with Stuart coincided with establishing myself in private practice, so life became extremely busy. Long days at the office were frequently capped off with dinner dates, and my days passed by in a chaotic blur. Perhaps that's why the two years I spent living in Maylands were uneventful as far as the other side was concerned. My sensitivity was dulled by my frenetic, full-on lifestyle, and I was loving every minute of it!

Although I still carried the after-effects of the haunting, with each ghost-free year that passed I felt increasingly bolstered, so much so that I decided to buy a house of my own, an old 1930s cottage on the Mount Lawley Avenues.

I wondered how I'd cope without the security of being surrounded by my neighbouring friends. The Maylands apartment had provided me with the best of both worlds: I had privacy and independence, but also knew that com-

Home delivery: With two black eyes and a broken nose, my future husband was delivered to my doorstep. This photo was taken a day or so before Stuart and I met. Despite his rough appearance, I was hooked!

pany was always close at hand should I need it. By moving to Mount Lawley, I would be entirely alone.

I moved into my three-bedroom cottage in the spring of 1996. I was delighted with it, despite feeling nervous about living alone. Because it was so old, I couldn't help worrying that I might be sharing my house with a ghost.

Two months after I moved in, confirmation of my uninvited housemate presented itself in spectacular fashion. It was around 11:00 PM when I settled into bed for the night, tired after a hectic day at work. I was just about to doze off when I was roused by the sound of footsteps running across the floorboards, rapidly heading towards my bedroom.

Circa 1997: In between my two favourite boys in my new house in Mount Lawley. Stu is at the head of the table, and Deni is smiling beside me. My good friend Bev is in the forefront, and my brother-in-law Michael (who features in the Albany chapter) is opposite me.

At first I thought it must've been my cat, but quickly realised that the footfalls were too heavy to be that of my three-month-old Birman. Someone or something was obviously running, and I braced myself as they burst through my bedroom door. The footsteps abruptly stopped at my bedside, yet I saw nothing in the impenetrable darkness. There was a scratchy shuffle of feet beside my bed, as if a small child was waiting for my attention.

Needless to say, I was beside myself, and all my old fears bubbled up and burst forth in a girly, high-pitched scream. (I find it amusing that despite my terror, I had enough presence of mind to register how ridiculous I sounded!)

I wasted no time snapping on the bedside lamp, and in a matter of minutes I was dressed and out the door. I was disappointed with myself that after all these years I was still allowing myself to be frightened by ghosts, but I knew that if I stayed at home I would spend the night terrified and sleepless, with all the lights blazing.

But it's only a little kid, I tried to reason with myself, but somehow I found the concept of needy, ghostly children even scarier than adult ghosts!

I drove towards Stuart's house in Shenton Park, berating myself for my weakness and angry that my home was not the idyllic refuge I had hoped it would be. The night became even more eventful as I drove through a busy intersection a few kilometres short of my destination. A car belted straight through a red light. It was almost surreal as it sped straight into my path, and for a split second I was uncomprehending of the vehicle before me. It practically skimmed the bonnet of my car, coming so close to hitting me that I was in its slipstream as it whizzed by. There was no time to brake as our paths converged; it was all over in a matter of seconds.

I was so shaken by the near miss that I pulled over to the side of the road, forcing myself to breathe deeply whilst I regained my composure. Then I became furious for the second time that night, as my sense of security was once again challenged, both events seemingly beyond my control.

By the time I arrived at Stuart's, I was emotionally drained, the surge of adrenaline had ebbed, and I felt deflated. As I relived the events of the night, I realised that my fearfulness had nearly killed me. Had I remained at my house and not allowed fear to dominate me, I would not have placed myself in a life-threatening situation. I resolved to face my fears head-on, and reasoned that in all the encounters I'd had with the spirit world, I had always emerged unscathed. Perhaps it was time to stop fighting the spirits and accept them. Maybe then they wouldn't be so hell-bent on commandeering my attention.

I awoke the following morning feeling flat, still disbelieving that I had once again been unlucky enough to find myself living with a ghost. I still didn't realise that I was clairvoyant; I just thought I had chanced upon another haunted house.

I reminded myself of my resolve to be strong and tried to shake the feeling of being victimised. I was braced for my next encounter, little knowing that my next ghostly visitor would be one of my dearest friends.

Chapter Seven

Deni

On a rainy night in 1997, Stuart and I became engaged, the result of Stu's spur-of-the-moment wedding proposal whilst waiting for the traffic lights to change. Although it was always a foregone conclusion that we would marry, our family and friends were delighted when we officially announced our impending wedding for the following April. Deni was particularly happy for us, having stamped big-brotherly approval on Stuart from the moment they first met. Stuart was similarly taken with Deni, and I often joked that they were a mutual admiration society.

Our eight-month engagement passed by in a blur, as I was consumed by the chaos of planning our wedding. In the last few weeks I was frantically chasing RSVPs, needing to finalise numbers before confirming with the function centre.

In typically slack fashion, our wedding day loomed without word from Deni, so I called to ask if he and his girlfriend, Taryn, would be attending. Taryn answered the phone and told me he was in the shower. She walked into the bathroom and I could hear Deni's voice echoing over the rushing water: "Barbarich! Tell her I'll call her back!" Taryn assured me they would be at the wedding in a month's time, and that she would get Deni to call me as soon as he had finished his shower.

"Don't worry about it," I said. "Tell him he doesn't need to call. I just wanted to make sure you guys were coming."

"For sure," she said. "See you on the big day!"

And I've regretted that conversation ever since, because in one blasé moment, I relinquished the opportunity to speak to my dearest friend for the very last time. The following weekend he was dead.

I found out via my answering machine, three weeks before my wedding. Taryn was breathless, almost inaudible. "Deni's dead," she sobbed. "H…His plane crashed…I'll…I'll call later." I stood frozen, trembling. I couldn't comprehend what I was hearing; I couldn't believe an answering machine had just delivered such shattering news. I replayed it. Maybe I'd misheard; maybe he'd survived. I played the message over and over, uncomprehending. *People don't leave this kind of news on answering machines, do they? It's got to be some kind of joke! Surely Deni's going to ring me any minute? Bloody Deni with his sick sense of humour! Maybe he put Taryn up to it.*

I grasped at straws, but of course I knew it was real. After the shock subsided I broke down, wracked with grief, numbed by incomprehension. How could this be real? Worse still, it hit me that the joy flight in a vintage biplane was in celebration of Deni's thirtieth birthday, and the grief slapped me in the face anew.

Deni's funeral was a packed-out affair. There was a large contingency of glamorous-looking babes, and I couldn't help but think that Deni would be delighted. The mourners spilt out of the vestibule and onto the church steps. The steady sound of crying accompanied the entire service, and I found myself breaking down every time I glanced up at his coffin. Emotion reached a peak at the final blessing, as Deni's best buddies moved towards the coffin to carry him out of the church in his last farewell. The priest signalled for the music to begin.

The church was suddenly transformed into a pseudo-nightclub, as the raucous strains of Deni's favourite song blasted through the church at full volume. The lyrics extolled the virtues of nightclubbing and getting drunk. The words of the chorus struck a chord despite their rancour, a repetitive chant about *getting knocked down and getting up again, and never being kept down*. They almost had us believing that Deni would burst out of his casket at any minute, declaring that he hadn't actually died at all.

The priest was scandalized and rushed toward the PA system, abruptly signalling for the music to be turned off. He thought there had been a mistake, and was horrified that the funeral had been spoilt by the tasteless music that had inadvertently thundered through his church. There was a whispered exchange between the priest and the pallbearers, and after a few minutes Deni's favourite song started up again.

As it played we found ourselves both laughing and crying, silently congratulating whoever chose Deni's swan song, because without a doubt, he would have absolutely loved it.

First Signs

Our wedding two weeks later was a joyous celebration, in spite of our recent loss. I had no idea how I would handle Deni's absence on the day, but was glad that love, hope, and positivity for the future overrode our sorrow. I felt sure that Deni was somehow still with us, and Stuart made sure he was remembered in the speeches.

Stuart and I both knew that Deni would have been mortified if we had allowed his death to spoil our wedding day, and were proud that we had managed to keep our sorrow at bay. But once the festivities were over and life settled back into a routine, the pain crept back and refused to budge.

By the time Deni died, I had been closed off from the spirit world for almost ten years, partly due to my sensitivity being dulled by the distractions of my busy lifestyle. But even more so, my lingering fears were blocking any possibility of developing my clairvoyance. I resolutely built a wall of protection around myself and rejected anything connected to the paranormal. I didn't think for a moment that interacting with spirits could be a positive experience that I would ultimately embrace.

*Stuart and I, with glandular fever, black eyes,
and broken noses behind us. Sixteen years on,
at my fortieth birthday celebration!*

Although my memories of the Kensington ghosts remained
vivid, I managed to control my fears to the point where they no
longer dominated my every waking thought. I felt that the dark
days were behind me and that I had somehow regained control. I was in the mindset that the ghosts had been left behind
in Kensington, and tried to convince myself that there was no
need to fear them.

Whilst keeping my fear in check deprived any opportu-
nistic ghosts of a potential power source, I also was inadvertently blocking any possibility of developing my spiritual
gifts.

I had very few paranormal experiences during most of
my twenties, and that was the way I wanted it. But something
within me changed when Deni died; the barrier dropped just
a little, and I couldn't help wondering if my friend was still
around.

Looking back now, I believe it was Deni's death that
facilitated the resurgence of my clairvoyant abilities, which

thankfully resumed very differently from the experiences of my youth. Perhaps the spirit world knew that if my reawakening bore any resemblance to the encounters of my teen years, I would retreat into my shell and block my clairvoyance forever.

The most important factor that allowed me to lower my guard was that the spirit trying to make contact was Deni. The thought of a loved one in spirit form was of course much less threatening than an unrecognised, random presence, so despite my remaining fears, I found myself actually hoping for a sign from my friend.

At first I was so consumed with grief that every memory of Deni had me bursting into tears. But as time went on, and my fears began to dissipate, I wished more and more for a connection to be made.

It seemed as though my wishing was all the encouragement Deni needed, as it wasn't long before I started to feel his presence. Although my first impulse was to be scared at the thought of a ghost being around, I tried not to let my fears sabotage any possible contact between us. I reminded myself that it was only Deni, mucking around and having a bit of fun as he had done in life. It took a bit of convincing, but as time went on I felt progressively more comfortable in his presence.

It began with the radio turning itself on; in true Deni-style it came on much louder than Stu or I would listen to it, and it was tuned to Deni's favourite radio station, Triple J. I desperately wanted to believe this was a sign, but I needed more.

A few days later I was home alone cleaning the house while Stu was playing cricket. I walked back into the master bedroom that I had just vacuumed, and noticed my bedside drawer had been opened. I was taken aback, knowing the drawer had been closed only a minute or so earlier. Feeling just a little apprehensive, I walked over to shut it when I noticed a card sitting at the very top. It was a card from Deni, which he had given me several years earlier. I had forgotten all about it, and seeing it again made my heart skip a beat.

I opened it with trembling hands. It read: "Barbs, Happy Birthday and make sure I'm invited over at least 100 times for dinner. Deni xxx." Transcribing it now, I can't help but laugh, as I know that whether or not he'd been invited, Deni would've turned up for dinner a hundred times anyway!

From then on, I often felt his comforting presence and had little doubt that Deni was around. Despite my happiness at the validations Deni had offered, I still found myself hindered by my fears. I told Deni that I was happy to have him around as long as he didn't show himself!

Deni conceded to my wishes, making his presence known in subtle and amusing ways whilst stopping short of actually manifesting before me. The spirit contact gradually developed to the point that whenever Deni was around, I'd see a bright flashing light. I reminded him that a light was fine, but under no circumstances was he to appear as a figure. The more I tuned in to Deni's presence, the more I seemed to experience, to the point that I was seeing auras and flashing lights pretty much wherever I went.

Of course at times I wondered if I was deluding myself, and questioned whether Deni's persistent presence was all just a case of wishful thinking. I found reassurance in the fact that I was consistently seeing auras and flashing lights, so I told myself that *surely I was tuned in clairvoyantly.* This at least temporarily put my mind at rest, until it occurred to me that there may have been a medically based explanation for my visions.

Once the thought entered my head, I couldn't accept a paranormal explanation for my recent experiences until I'd excluded all possible physiological possibilities first. Being a scientist, I was trained to seek the most rational explanation, so I finally booked in for a full medical examination a few weeks later.

I presented to the local medical centre complaining of "visual disturbances," not wanting to taint my professional reputation by stating outright that I was seeing auras and bright flashing lights. Having eliminated the possibility of a brain tumour or stroke, the general physician suspected a detached retina and promptly despatched me to an ophthalmologist. When these results all reported to be in order, the doctor wiped his hands of me and assured me all was fine and "not to worry about it."

Once I had the medical all clear, I was willing to accept that what I was experiencing was indeed paranormal. This was the first time I acknowledged that I had extrasensory abilities, and I was desperate to know more.

My first port of call was a local clairvoyant, a lady called Dawn whose reputation promised great things. Although the reading itself was not the insightful revelation I had hoped for, her practical advice proved invaluable in steering me in the right direction. Dawn recommended expanding my knowledge through reading and meditation, and suggested attending a Spiritualist church. She told me that the combined energies of like-minded people would enhance my visions and possibly provide the answers I was looking for.

So within the week, I attended my first service at a Spiritualist church, on a befittingly wild and wintery night.

Reawakening

I'm not sure what I was expecting, but the Forrestfield Spiritualist Church was not what I had imagined. Firstly, it was not a church at all, but a large fluoro-lit room in a white brick community centre. Orange plastic chairs were arranged in rows of about twenty, with a pine lectern at the front. A decrepit-looking upright piano sat to the right, and a Formica table laden with mismatched coffee mugs and an urn sat on the left. Surprisingly normal-looking people filtered in quietly, with nary a hippy, New Age type to be seen.

Admittedly I didn't have high hopes for the evening. I really wanted to believe that the Spiritualist church would help me understand my recent experiences, but I couldn't help my preconceived prejudices from clouding my judgement. The whole concept seemed somehow forced and foreign to me. The effusive welcoming smiles of the church regulars seemed just that little bit *too nice*, and it wasn't long before my cynical side kicked in.

It was a Wednesday evening and as eight o'clock struck, there was a collective clearing of throats as a small, gnarly granny seated herself at the piano. With a sideward glance she smiled and nodded at the congregation as the piano clattered into life. I had to restrain the urge to snigger as she launched into a flowery rendition of an overplayed '70s pop song about believing in angels.

Good Lord, spare me, I thought, as the congregation chimed in. I was almost contemplating escape when I felt a sharp tug on the back of my jumper, and this proved to be the turning point of my night. As I spun around to see who was not so subtly trying to get my attention, I was gobsmacked to see that there was no one in the row behind me.

Denovich! I immediately thought, and suddenly I was happy to stay, curious to discover what more this night had to offer.

I tried to dismiss the clichéd songs that were interspersed throughout the service, and even found myself mouthing the words to some of the reinvented pop songs as the service dragged on.

I had little interest in the *philosophy* component; I was hearing nothing new and was impatient for the display of clairvoyance to begin. I was dismayed when the pianist granny shuffled to the lectern and announced that we had a *special treat* prior to the clairvoyance.

"Janice has returned to our fold and wishes to share with us briefly what has been going on in her life for the past few months."

I suppressed a groan as a mousy-looking woman in her early fifties slowly made her way to the front. She was dressed in what I imagined to be her "church best" but was in fact an unflattering pale blue skirt and jacket ensemble, with a faded floral T-shirt underneath. By now I was impatient to get home, and paid little regard to what Janice was saying.

Needless to say, her temporary absence from the flock had been fraught with unhappiness and misfortune. She began to cry as she relayed the events of the last few months, including the death of her mother. All at once she had my undivided attention, as I suddenly noticed the brilliant flashing lights that surrounded her. It was the lights that had led me to the church in the first place, and I was desperate to discover what they meant.

I could no longer hear what Janice was saying as I became totally transfixed by her aura, a luminescent pale green colour that appeared to shoot upwards from her crown. Although I had seen the flashing lights so often before, this time they were different. They were brighter and more insistent; they were changing.

Suddenly the lights transformed into two pale white figures and my heart began to race as I watched the spirits materialise before me. To say that I was awestruck would not do my emotions justice—I was completely blown away.

One of the spirits stood behind Janice and was a good head taller; he was large and dominant, and wrapped his arms around her in a gesture so protective it brought tears to my eyes. To Janice's left, a shorter, stockier figure moved in close beside her, extending his right arm and placing it around her shoulders.

I looked to the people around me in awe. *Was anyone else seeing this?* I was emotional and humbled. In the minute or two that I observed these beings, I was struck by the realisation that we are never truly alone and that the world in which we live is so much more beautiful than we could ever imagine.

Then, as suddenly as they appeared, the figures faded. The world would never look the same to me again, and I knew beyond a doubt that Deni had been instrumental in the reawakening of my clairvoyance. Contrary to what I had expected, seeing spirits was not even remotely scary; the experience made me feel more protected than ever. I needn't have issued Deni all those warnings after all!

As I reflect on these events now, I can't imagine a gentler way for me to be shown that the flashing lights around people are in fact entities. Seeing spirits again for the first time since I was a teenager left me feeling happy and awestruck. After all, if I was seeing the flashing lights around most people I came into contact with, did this mean we were all surrounded by these loving, gentle spirits? The thought of it filled me with joy.

It was on this night that I abandoned my deeply rooted fear of spirits, as I realised that we are all more loved and protected than I ever thought possible. After sixteen years of fearing the spirit world, I was finally ready to move on.

Chapter Eight

Meditation

I was so excited by my newly discovered clairvoyance that I immersed myself in as much relevant reading as possible. I loved relating to other people's experiences and comparing them to my own. They seemed to validate that what I was experiencing was not only life-enhancing but also very real.

It was around this time that I began to meditate, so as to still my mind and make myself more receptive to the subtle energies around me. I began using a technique that makes use of a clear quartz crystal to open the third eye and enhance clairvoyant vision. At first I found it difficult to remember the sequence of visualisations that the technique employed, but by my third or fourth attempt I had practiced enough to let the meditative sequence flow.

Perhaps a little strangely, I have always preferred to meditate with my eyes open, as when I close my eyes I feel as though I might miss seeing something. My logic tells me this is ridiculous, as I know that my clairvoyant visions are being perceived by my third eye and not my physical eyes, but it is now an ingrained habit and very hard to break.

I suppose it all stems from my early eyes-closed meditations, when I didn't entirely trust the visions that would suddenly appear before me. I worried that the images were of my own creation, as after all, *I was only seeing them in my head!*

If, however, my eyes were open, I trusted the visions more, as I was seeing real figures in the real world rather than just in my mind. As such, I decided to meditate with my eyes open, and have done so ever since.

I always enjoy reliving the memory of my first successful meditation, as I believe it was the first time I made contact with my spirit guide. As I lay on the bed holding my crystal, I noticed a pale green light slowly pulsing in the corner of the bedroom. I was mesmerised by its slow, deliberate flash, and each time it reappeared, it had moved a little closer. It didn't take long for it to cross the room, and in less than a minute it was pulsing right in front of my face.

I was able to put my fingers through its luminescent green glow and rest it in the palm of my hand; the whole experience was exhilarating. Half of me wanted to jump up and down with excitement, whilst the other half just felt extremely relaxed as I allowed myself to savour the moment.

Whenever I do this meditation, the soothing green light never fails to appear, and stays with me for as long as I maintain my state of relaxation. It has been a constant in my journey and consistently calms me, hence my assumption that it is likely to be my guide.

Discovering Orbs

In addition to my regular meditations, I voraciously consumed every scrap of information about the paranormal that I could get my hands on. Every once in a while I would come across the subject of orbs, and I was more than a little intrigued.

Orbs are thought to be manifestations of spirit energy and appear in photographs as glowing balls of light. The more I read, the more excited I became, as at last there seemed to be a way to validate the existence of the bright spirit lights I was seeing every day.

I began by following the advice of the paranormal authors, and set aside regular times for my orb-hunting expeditions. I would voice an invitation for any spirits present to make themselves known, and then take the photo whilst in the mindset that I was photographing spirits rather than the people or the material objects before me.

I soon amassed a comprehensive collection of orb photos, demonstrating orbs of various shapes, colours, intensities, and sizes.

As skeptics are quick to point out, it's true that orbs can often be attributed to explainable physical events, such as when light reflects off airborne dust, small insects, or water droplets. However, since I was frequently seeing the spirit lights prior to taking the photos, I was sure that my photographs were indeed showing the real deal. To inspire the same confidence in whoever was with me at the time, I would tell them where the spirit was and then quickly snap the photo to prove it. The physical artefact theory could then be discounted, as it was highly unlikely that a dust particle or water droplet had suddenly placed itself in the very position where I had just claimed to see a spirit.

As people with clairvoyant abilities well know, there is often an air of skepticism when you tell someone that there is a spirit in the room. But if you can produce a photo with an orb as added ammunition, the claim immediately takes on more substance. Whereas I used to just say "You have a spirit with you today," I am now more likely to substantiate what I am seeing by reaching for my camera. Having something concrete to show someone, rather than just a succession of claims, is certainly gratifying.

Chapter Nine

Giulia

By 2001 I had completely embraced my growing clairvoy-ance, and had all but cast aside my residual fears. By now Stuart and I had become parents, with the arrival of Eloise in 1999 and Claire twenty months later. Waiting in the wings was our son, Daniel, who completed our family in 2005.

Even though I was busy raising our young family, I man-aged to continue consulting at my clinic for a few hours each week. My clinic provided me with the opportunity to keep my professional profile and maintain my practical skills, and also proved to be a stomping ground for the occasional ghost or spirit.

In the early days after reconnecting with the spirit world, Deni's presence was an unwavering constant. It didn't take long for him to view my recent spiritual awakening as his green light, and it was just a matter of time before he chose to appear to me. Ever the pot stirrer, Deni would more often than not show himself to me at my clinic, usually in front of patients when I was least able to react.

Every Friday afternoon, I would see a young man languishing in an armchair in the corner of my consulting room, right beside the patient I was treating. My clairvoyant vision at the time was such that I could see pale white figures, but little detail. I could differentiate their sex, height, body type, and occasionally their hairline, but not much else. Although I couldn't make out his facial features, his sturdy build was unmistakable and I had no doubt that my regular Friday afternoon visitor was Deni, especially since in our uni days the Friday afternoon visit to the tavern had been quite a ritual.

I didn't realise that confirmation was on its way; and as with most of life's pivotal moments, it came when it was least expected.

It was a Friday afternoon when Giulia first attended my clinic for an appointment. Unbeknownst to me at the time, Giulia is a gifted clairvoyant and has been communicating with spirits since she was a small child living in Italy.

She is a classic *Italian mama*, with a Rubenesque plumpness that makes her all the more endearing. Her flashing brown eyes lock with your own when you speak to her, leaving no doubt that she is completely engaged and interested in what you are saying.

Despite a difficult life, Giulia gives the impression of not having a care in the world, which I have since discovered is a direct result of her spiritual gifts. She laughs at the drop of a

*Everyone should have a Giulia
in their lives! As well as being a
gifted medium, Giulia is a joyous
soul who brings love and light
to everyone around her. Giulia
has been a loving mentor on my
spiritual journey.*

hat and is generous to a fault. Everyone should have a Giulia
in their lives! I treasure the memories of the day we met, as
she has since become a much-loved family friend.

I've often wondered whether Deni played a role in the
blossoming of our friendship, as he made sure he was there
when Giulia first came to my clinic. I suppose my surrepti-
tious glances towards Deni in his corner weren't as subtle as I
imagined, as it wasn't long before Giulia looked over her left
shoulder to see what I kept looking at. From that moment
the energy in the room skyrocketed, as Deni, Giulia, and I
were overtaken by excitement.

"Oh my God!" she gasped, and then started laughing.
"Who *is* that?"

We were both momentarily stunned to discover we could both see spirits, and there was an instant connection between us. Giulia was excited to connect with the cheeky young man beside her, I was thrilled to have Deni's identity confirmed, and Deni was delighted to be noticed!

Giulia went on to describe Deni in great detail, right down to his twinkling brown eyes and face-splitting grin. She described his tragic death, and said that despite Deni's initial shock at being *wiped out* at such a young age, he realised it was his time and was now happy to be involved in his loved ones' lives from the other side.

It is now over thirteen years since Deni died, and his Friday afternoon visits have dwindled. It feels as though once he fulfilled his objective, he stepped back to assume a more subtle role in my life, as his guidance was no longer needed. He supported me through the painful aftermath of his death and helped to reawaken my clairvoyant abilities. He helped me to let go of my overwhelming fears so I could embrace life wholly and without reservation, and for that I am especially grateful.

He showed me that the pain of losing a loved one can eventually give way to joyfulness and gratitude for having had someone so wonderful in our lives. Deni convinced me that the bonds of love remain regardless of what happens to the body, and that the spirit never dies.

These days when I think of Deni, I'm hard-pressed to feel sad. The feelings his memory evokes are invariably joyful; he just got to where we're all going a little sooner than the rest of us. And I'm sure that suits him fine.

House of Spirits

We moved into our current family home in Kalamunda in June of 2001. Kalamunda is a bushland suburb nestled in the Perth Hills offering a quiet village lifestyle despite its proximity to the city. We felt as though we were living in the countryside even though the bustle of Perth was a mere twenty miles away.

Our new home had all the features we had been looking for in our twelve-month search for a bigger house, with polished wooden floors and views across the valley. My only concern was the fact that it was double storey, with a perilous set of stairs.

Since Eloise was now an active two-year-old (and it was just a matter of time before Claire started toddling after her sister), the first thing we did upon moving in was to install a childproof gate at the top of the stairwell. Despite its presence I always felt apprehensive, and Stuart and I insisted that Eloise always go down the stairs on her bottom.

When the excitement of moving in wore off, I started to notice a presence in the downstairs family room. The more relaxed I became in my new surroundings, the more I tuned in to the house's energy. It didn't take long to realise that not one but numerous spirits were occupying the room downstairs. I noticed that when I spent an extended length of time there, I ended up feeling very drained. I began to suspect that the previous owners were aware of the spirits in their home, thus explaining its surprisingly affordable purchase price, even offering to drop the price by a further ten thousand dollars to hasten the sale.

As the months slipped by, I became increasingly aware of the presences; it felt as though there was a continuous stream of spirits convening in our family room. Whilst the energy didn't feel negative, it began to feel oppressive, and whenever I went downstairs it felt as though I was walking into a dense fog. The room was thick with the fuzz of vibration and constant flashing lights.

One day the unthinkable happened, and my fears were realised as Eloise tumbled down the entire flight of stairs. I was in my bedroom when I heard the gate squeak open, followed by the sickening thuds of her body thumping down the wooden staircase.

My mother-in-law reached the top of the stairwell first; she was screaming and helpless. I was a shaking mess as I scrambled after my daughter, who by now was lying limp at the bottom. I rolled her over carefully; her face was tear-stained and bloody from where her teeth had bitten through her lip. My eyes scanned her limbs and, satisfied she had not broken anything, I scooped her into my arms. Claire had been spared the drama as she safely slept in her cot, but my mother-in-law and I cried together with Eloise as we tried to process our shock.

Within half an hour, Eloise was perfectly fine, and except for a bump on her head and a fat lower lip, it was as if nothing had happened. She was more traumatised by the general physician who paid a housecall later that afternoon, a buf-

My children—(L–R) Claire, Daniel, and Eloise—pictured on the famous stairs. Despite taking significant tumbles on them, somehow our children always emerged unscathed.

foon who scared his young patient before the examination even began.

"Who's fallen down the stairs then?" he boomed as he walked through the front door. "Where's the naughty girl who opened up the kiddie gate?"

I expect this was an attempt at humour, but Eloise cowered under her bedclothes until we assured her she was not in trouble. The doctor confirmed that she was unharmed, and was thankfully soon on his way.

A few weeks later, I ran into Giulia. I hadn't seen her since Eloise's accident, so I was a little taken aback when she asked me if someone had had a serious fall.

"Eloise fell down the stairs about a month ago," I told her. "Why?"

"Well, there is a man here, your old uncle from Croatia… he's telling me he caught her. She didn't get hurt, did she?"

"Not really," I said, "considering she fell down an entire flight of stairs…"

"Well, you can thank your uncle for that!" she smiled.

Despite never having visited my house, Giulia went on to tell me about a downstairs room that was teeming with spirits. "They all gather around your bar area!" I immediately felt a shiver down my spine, as Giulia had just confirmed what I had suspected all along. "They were attracted by the previous owner," she told me. "Apparently she was some kind of healer."

It all fell into place as I recalled the first time I had inspected the house. The downstairs room was decorated with esoteric pictures, and an Indonesian-style table was laden with small liquid-filled bottles in every conceivable colour. There was also an impressive collection of crystals, and the smell of incense wafted up the stairwell.

I later discovered the house was used as a bed and breakfast that focussed on spiritual healing. The previous owners called it "Anahata Retreat," which they named after the heart chakra. It was also used as a meditation centre, and hosted weekly classes for the purposes of spiritual enlightenment.

I arranged for Giulia to come for dinner a couple weeks later. As she descended the hazardous staircase (replaced soon after by wider, carpeted stairs), she was overwhelmed by the energy in the room. Despite its spaciousness she suddenly felt claustrophobic; she broke into a sweat and struggled to breathe.

"Oh dear!" she gasped. "This place may have been used for healing, but all the baggage has been left behind." She glanced toward the bar area and suddenly started giggling. "You've got quite a selection of ghosts here!" She pointed towards a pair of nuns who stood alongside a trio dressed in Victorian garb. Beside them were a couple of hippies. She told me they were functioning on the astral plane and were totally unaware of our presence.

Although they posed no threat, Giulia stressed that it was important to move the spirits on, as they were affecting the energy balance in our household. Possessing clairvoyant abilities made me particularly vulnerable to their presence, which explained why I felt constantly drained.

Giulia advised me to cleanse the house, so I bought a large smudge stick the following day. A smudge stick is a bundle of dried herbs (usually white sage) that is used for clearing negative or residual energy.

Giulia suggested that I open all the doors and windows and waft the pungent smoke into every corner whilst mindful of the intention of cleansing the house. I also filled my oil burners with house-clearing oils, and it didn't take long for the atmosphere to lift.

Although I feel confident that the lingering energies from the previous owners have now moved on, I still find that our home is highly attractive to spirits. It is a combination of its history and the legacy of those who have passed through its doors. But I imagine it is mostly because they know that here they will be acknowledged and accepted with love.

I am comforted by these presences, which usually radiate a sense of positivity and protection. Especially since, seven years after Eloise hurtled down the stairs, our family was shaken by a sickening case of history repeating itself, and I feel sure that some intervention from the spirit world averted a potentially tragic accident.

In typically exuberant two-year-old fashion, our son, Daniel, dislodged the entire safety gate and rode it down the stairs whilst lying on his stomach paddleboard style. From where I sat in the kitchen, all I could hear was the clattering thud of the metal gate as it skidded down the stairs, accompanied by the synchronised screams of my two panicked daughters.

By the time I reached the top of the stairs a few seconds later, Daniel was dusting himself off at the bottom, hands on hips as he nonchalantly stepped off the skewed metal gate. He kept repeating "I'm all right!" to reassure me (and undoubtedly himself) that all was well.

For a long time afterwards, I could see a white light bathing the top of the stairwell, assuring me that the stairs would pose no further threat to my children, regardless of how recklessly they behaved.

Spirit Man

My revived clairvoyance was mostly exciting but also a little daunting. Whilst the majority of my experiences left me happily awestruck, occasionally my deep-rooted fears would leap up and confront me.

One night I was sitting alone in the upstairs lounge room watching TV as Stuart was working the night shift. By this time he had left my brother's law firm and had retrained as a professional firefighter, so I had to adapt to being alone with the children for the twice-weekly night shifts.

I had long abandoned sitting in the downstairs family room alone at night, as I still found it to be a thoroughfare for the occasional passing spirit. I didn't expect anyone to follow me into my upstairs sanctuary, but on this particular evening that's exactly what one of the spirits did!

It began when I looked down at my crossed legs and noticed my aura. It was little more than a fuzzy luminescence extending an inch or so from my body, and as I looked at it I felt excited and intrigued. I held up my hand against the green wall, and saw the same white glow emanating from each of my fingers.

Nowadays when I see auras, I know that I have tuned in to spirit energy, and as such I expect to see something more. Back then, though, I'd seen auras on only a handful of occasions and hadn't yet established this link, so I was taken aback when my vision developed further.

From the corner of my eye I could see a bright flashing light; it was on my right, no more than four or five feet away. I knew without a doubt that someone was there, but steadfastly refused to look. I knew that if I saw a spirit in the room, I would feel uneasy for the rest of the night, especially since I was alone with the children.

Flash! Flash! Flash! *Not looking...* Flash! I still refused to look. Flash! *Okay then*, I thought, as it seemed as though whoever was there wouldn't go away until they'd been acknowledged.

I turned to my right to see a tall, upright man. He was facing away from me, looking towards the television. He was a glowing pearlescent white and radiated a quiet easiness, as if he felt perfectly at home. Although he wasn't threatening, his presence still made me uncomfortable.

"Hi," I said nervously, "I can see you…" He continued to stare at the TV (just like any other man would, I guess). "I'm sorry, but you're frightening me. Would you please leave?"

I felt ridiculous, mostly for talking out loud to a filmy figure I wasn't even sure could hear me, but also for allowing myself to be scared.

"You're welcome to come back in the daytime or when Stuart's home… It's just that I feel nervous when I'm on my own."

The man instantly faded, and in his place a pinprick of bright light hovered above the floor. It burst into a cascading explosion of light, shooting directly towards me like a firecracker. It lasted for no more than a few seconds and felt like a goodbye.

My fears were all but forgotten as I headed to bed that evening, feeling comforted and blessed. I was increasingly accepting that there is nothing to fear from spirits, and wondered if in fact the opposite was true. Would it make more sense to be fearful if they were *not* around? It dawned on me that the spirits are my protectors, that I am surrounded by their love. I slept soundly that night, for the first time since Stuart started working night shifts.

The Paranormal Psychologist

As my ability to see spirits became more finely tuned, I found it increasingly frustrating that I was rarely able to hear them.

Whilst I felt that many of them wanted nothing more than to be acknowledged, I had no doubt that some of the spirits were trying to convey a message to their loved ones.

It was this mounting frustration that led me to seek out an appointment with Janet Cromwell, a renowned paranormal psychologist who specialises in the assessment and development of psychic abilities. When I called to make the appointment, she assured me that she would be able to "switch on my clairaudience," thereby allowing any messages from the spirit world to come through.

After a three-week wait for an appointment, I found myself ushered into Dr. Cromwell's office, and was seated directly opposite her. There was no desk between us, just a small coffee table with a box of tissues placed on it. I had no idea what to expect and suddenly felt extremely vulnerable.

I looked up to see two spirits standing slightly behind Dr. Cromwell, one to either side of her. They were burly, masculine figures, and as I looked at them, Dr. Cromwell indicated over her shoulders with her thumbs.

"That's John and that's Cyril. They're my spirit guides. I know you can see them. You're *not* crazy. Now let's get to work!"

She joked about how disappointing it was to discover their lacklustre names, having imagined names infinitely more exotic. Her cockney English accent made her seem down-to-earth and approachable, and I soon relaxed into what turned out to be a mammoth three-hour session.

I told her about my teenage experiences with poltergeists, and about the figures who had appeared beside my bed.

While she accepted that I had seen numerous entities during this period, she suggested that the actual physical phenomena may have been manifestations of my own psychic energy rather than vengeful spirits trying to attack me. This notion was comforting and was certainly a possibility I was willing to entertain, although I didn't believe that all the disturbances could have been of my own creation.

Dr. Cromwell led me through a guided meditation, ostensibly to introduce me to my spirit guide and open up the possibility of communication between myself and the spiritual dimensions. I saw my guide standing across a narrow rushing river, yet I couldn't find a bridge to reach him.

In accordance with my usual clairvoyant visions, he was a hazy white figure and I was unable to see his face. I called out to him and asked him his name; he was present but silent. Or I suppose he may have been calling back but I just couldn't hear him!

"Stop trying so hard," said Dr. Cromwell in her hypnotic, level voice. "Just relax and listen…What is he saying?"

I dropped deeper into my meditation but still received nothing. After what felt like an inordinate length of time, she guided me back to full consciousness. Despite a deep sense of calm, there was a tinge of disappointment, as I felt my quest for clairaudience had failed.

Unwilling to give up, Dr. Cromwell wanted to delve deeper into the experiences of my youth, thinking that perhaps there was some lingering fear that was blocking my progression. She began to question me, and it was soon obvious which direction the conversation was taking.

"Have you ever had a fear of clowns?"

"No," I laughed. "I can't say that clowns have ever particularly worried me!"

"What about sleeping next to doors or windows? Does that worry you?" I was momentarily confused, but it soon became clear what she was getting at. "Have you ever woken in the morning to find strange wounds or markings on your body?"

As I looked around Dr. Cromwell's office it suddenly dawned on me. *My God! She's checking to see if I've been abducted by aliens!* There were subtle indicators of Dr. Cromwell's fascination with extraterrestrials around her office, from the book titles on her shelf to the small busts of pear-headed aliens that sat alongside them. There was a painting of a spaceship against a starry sky backdrop and a stand of leaflets titled *Alien Abduction: It Can Happen to You!*

I managed to convince Dr. Cromwell that I hadn't had any contact with aliens, and couldn't help but feel that she was somewhat disappointed that I wasn't an abductee. We said our farewells and I left, feeling both bemused and a little let down.

A few nights later, something happened that made me rethink the results of my appointment, and I wondered if the three-hour session may have been a success after all. Just as I was getting into bed, I heard a voice, as clearly as though someone was in the room with me. It was my friend Lane, who had moved to Melbourne a month earlier with her husband and three children.

"Barbie!" she said, "I'm pregnant!" I looked around the room, momentarily stunned and disoriented. For a split second I couldn't work out what was going on, and then it hit me that perhaps this was a psychic message.

The following morning I decided to throw caution to the wind and sent Lane the following text message: "Hi Lane, R U pregnant? Cos last night I distinctly heard you in my bedroom telling me so…x" The phone rang almost immediately.

"You are seriously weird, Barbie… Stop freaking me out!" It turned out Lane took the pregnancy test that very day, and must have been subconsciously sending the news to me via the ether.

I have no doubt that Lane and I share some kind of psychic link, as she has on occasion tapped into my thoughts as well. When I gave birth to my son, Daniel, a week early, Lane rang me first thing the following morning, convinced my baby had been born during the night!

I feel that all friends and family share a psychic connection; the closer we are emotionally, the stronger the telepathic link. It is the clutter of thoughts and constant activity of modern life that cloud our psychic abilities.

Despite this sudden burst of clairaudience, I have remained pretty much deaf to the voices of spirits. I have had to rely largely on my visions to facilitate communication, which, fortunately for me, have continued to remain strong.

Part Two

The
Interactions

Chapter Ten

Deni's Legacy

As a result of my gradual reintroduction into the spirit world, I embraced my revived abilities with appreciation and calm. I seemed to be at my most receptive when I was at my podiatry practice, where I was free from the distractions and chaos that come with being a mother of three.

Rare was the patient who came into my clinic without a spirit or two in tow, and I found I was constantly distracted by my patients' glowing auras. My workday was rich with continual reminders of how intrinsically bound the spirit world is to our own, and it made me view the world with a renewed sense of appreciation.

My quandary has always been whether to reveal my abilities or to keep them private. I was well aware that if I divulged everything I was seeing, it wouldn't be long before I developed a reputation as a fruitcake and my professional standing would be compromised. As such, I adopted the strategy of mentally acknowledging spirits when I saw them. I would telepathically say "Hi, I see you!" without voicing anything in front of the patient before me. That way I retained my professionalism as a podiatrist without ignoring the spirits who seemed so delighted that I could see them.

However, nothing is ever so cut and dried, and I have occasionally found myself in situations where I have had little choice but to put my pride aside and reveal what I am experiencing. I find this is particularly the case when I am dealing with spirit children. I find it very hard to not fully acknowledge a child who is desperate to let their parents know they are okay. In these situations I consider establishing some kind of link between parents and their children vastly more important than putting my professional reputation on the line. The following two chapters are accounts of such experiences, where spirit children have reached out to me and I have found it impossible to say no.

Jack

It's hard to remain impartial about someone when the person is surrounded by spirits, especially when one of them is an impish little boy. This is what happened when I met Brad Marsden, a typically rugged-looking Aussie bloke. His spirit entourage was impressive, and as his appointment unfolded, the reason for this soon became clear.

It wasn't far into his session before Brad told me that his youngest son, Jack, had died three years earlier. Suddenly the energy in the room became palpable and I saw a little boy standing protectively beside his father. Just to make sure I noticed him, Jack repeatedly shone his bright spirit light at me, its camera-flash intensity sending a shiver down my spine each time. I was riding on a wave of extreme emotion as I was simultaneously sad and excited, the tragedy of Jack's passing allayed by the joyous affirmation that his spirit lives on.

I somehow managed to get through the foot assessment that Brad had come for, but once the business side of the appointment was over, we sat and talked for another half hour. In the brief time we spent together, Brad and I bonded more rapidly than new acquaintances usually do, and I couldn't help thinking that this was due largely to Jack.

I felt that I had no choice but to tell Brad what I was seeing, as I knew that jeopardising my professional reputation was inconsequential compared to the importance of him knowing that his son was still with him. Besides, despite having only just met him, I trusted Brad and knew he wouldn't judge me unfavourably.

Just before he left, Brad showed me a photo of Jack, and I was struck again by the same pang of concurrent sorrow and joy that I had felt earlier. I knew without a doubt that it was the same little boy I had just seen standing beside his father.

A few months later, Brad's wife, Angie, came by for an appointment, accompanied by her twin toddler daughters. She juggled a large nappy bag as she ushered her fair-haired little girls into my consulting room.

As in similar circumstances, I was in no doubt that something remarkable was about to happen. There was an unmistakable buzz in the air, and I braced myself for what I just knew would be a memorable visit.

The atmosphere was charged and the air felt thick with vibration. Angie's aura was radiant, and resplendent with flickers of bright lights that I now recognise as spirits. I tried to remain professional and focussed on the task at hand as I picked up my scalpel and set to work.

The conversation inevitably turned to family, and Angie told me about her eldest son's recent rugby triumphs. She spoke about her school-aged daughter, Olivia, and we laughed at the exploits of the twins.

Conversation then turned to Jack, and at the mention of his name, the flashing lights around Angie started to go berserk. Then, with one further comment, he was standing before me, a mischievous grin plastered on his face.

"I'm sure Jack's around me," Angie smiled, "and so is my dad." Not surprisingly, a large figure appeared behind her, resting his hand on young Jack's shoulder. My professionalism out the window, I placed my scalpel on the tray beside me. It was impossible to continue the appointment as if nothing had happened.

"You know what, Angie? You're absolutely right." When I told her what I was seeing, she didn't seem surprised.

It always touches me how closely linked family members remain after death, and I am always uplifted when those left behind are in tune enough to acknowledge their loved one's presence. Too often people are quick to dismiss their spiritual connection with those who have died, believing they may have just imagined it.

Angie told me that in the past when she has spoken about feeling Jack's presence, people were quick to assume her experiences were just a case of wishful thinking. I assured her that Jack was still beside her, and that she had been right in acknowledging his presence. She then had no hesitation in sharing her stories of affirmation that Jack is still very much around.

She told me how Jack plays tricks on his older brother, locking doors through which he has recently passed. The family has also returned home to discover toys strewn down the length of the hallway, despite the house being immaculate when they left. As the stories continued, Jack thrived on being the centre of attention, and continually flashed a blue light at me from the centre of his chest.

I have been told that this is the way spirits radiate love, and I was overwhelmed by the reciprocal love I was feeling for this little boy I had never physically met.

Since Jack knew I could see him, I wasn't entirely surprised when he followed me home. I had long since established that when a spirit knows I can see them, they gravitate towards me as a possible point of contact between themselves and their family.

Jack was particularly drawn to my son Daniel's room, and I was only slightly taken aback when my two-year-old asked me who the little boy is who watches him while he is sleeping. So when the siren of Dan's toy fire engine spontaneously roared into life at 2:00 AM, I immediately put it down to Jack.

Several weeks passed until Jack decided to take it one step further. Our house was pervaded by sadness, as our cat Willow had just died after being bitten by a snake. The children were devastated, and by the time I went to bed I was feeling emotionally drained.

Sometime after midnight I was awoken by a sudden thud on my chest, and the bed squeaked as though someone had just jumped onto it. I was momentarily terrified, as memories of my Kensington experiences came spontaneously flooding back.

I felt a face in the darkness just inches away from my own, hissing and spitting like a cat. Then I saw him, the same sweet face that I had seen a few days earlier in my clinic, and I knew straight away that it was Jack.

He stopped the hissing and began to laugh, a sweet child's chuckle that instantly dissolved my fears. With his face still right up against mine, I quietly giggled back into the darkness, as relief and a sense of peacefulness soon lulled me back to sleep.

Later when I relayed the story to my friend Linda, I told her that the episode left me feeling peaceful; however, I couldn't understand why Jack was hissing at me. "Ever occur to you he was pretending to be a cat? Maybe he wanted you to know he's been playing with Willow."

As soon as she said it, I knew she was right, as goose bumps coursed up and down my arms. I told the children and they felt better immediately, happy that their cat was not only safe from snakes but that she had a friend to play with!

Ivana and I: After consistently seeing Sarah's spirit light flashing above her mother's head, I asked her if she would like to appear in a photo. As this photograph attests, Sarah was more than happy to comply.

Sleeping Beauty

One of my most memorable spirit encounters involved a sixteen-year-old girl named Sarah, who accompanied her mother, Ivana, to her podiatry appointment.

I knew of Ivana long before I met her, as her husband, David, had been a patient at my clinic for some years. They had tragically lost their daughter Sarah five years earlier, and when I saw Ivana's name in my appointment diary, I couldn't help wondering if I would feel her daughter's presence.

Ivana was the last patient of the day on an overcast Thursday afternoon. An attractive blonde in her late forties, she smiled at me as I invited her into my treatment room.

We made small talk as I began her treatment, but all the while there was an unacknowledged energy between us, and I was filled with a familiar sense of expectation. My conviction that something was about to happen was reinforced as I glanced up at Ivana and took note of her strong white aura. It transiently flashed with tiny silver sparks.

The allotted half-hour treatment time was almost over before she made reference to Sarah, and set off a chain of events that will cement our friendship forever.

"Barbara," she said, her voice suddenly serious. "You know, sometimes I feel like there's someone around me…"

I was taken aback by the sudden turn in the conversation, and stupidly asked "Who do you think it is?" although I had no doubt to whom she was referring.

"I think it's Sarah," she said, "my daughter."

As I looked up, Ivana's aura pulsed, and then an enormous white light flashed above her head. It was too brilliant and intense to ignore and I found it impossible to hide my reaction. I was flung backwards on my chair as I stared at her incredulously.

"Well, you're obviously right," I said.

I momentarily debated whether to tell her what I had just seen, and decided that based on how I had reacted to the flash, she was already well aware that something was going on anyway.

"When you said you thought it was Sarah, there was an intense flash of white light above you. I'm sure it's her."

She studied me for a moment; it was hard to gauge her reaction.

"Really?" she said. "Wow."

I knew she wanted to believe me but didn't allow herself to get too excited. I got the feeling that despite the warmth she exuded, she remained guarded after having gone through so much. As she got up to leave, she turned to me and smiled.

"Thanks for telling me that." We embraced and then she was gone.

As I drove home that evening, I had a very strong sense of Sarah in the car with me. When I got home, I kept seeing a blue ball of light around me, particularly when I was playing with the children. The vivid blue light appeared as a slow deliberate flash, and radiated a sense of well-being.

For the next fortnight the blue light flitted around the house, sometimes transforming into a beautiful little figure, fleetingly passing through our hallway. I had no doubt that Sarah had followed me home, happy that I was aware of her presence.

One night some friends came for dinner, and the house was full of children, laughter, and music. We took turns singing karaoke, teasing one another, and getting progressively more raucous. We were thoroughly enjoying ourselves, and the more we laughed, the more vibrant the blue flashes of light became. I was sure that Sarah was with us, relishing the fun.

It was well after midnight by the time our guests left, and I had a quick shower before bed. A set of brightly painted porcelain drawers sits on top of the bathroom vanity, and as I dried myself I noticed that one of the drawers was wide open. Since the drawers are mostly for show and rarely used,

I was surprised to see it open, particularly since all six drawers had been closed when I got into the shower a few minutes earlier.

"Sarah," I said quietly, "if it's you, please open the drawer for me again." I closed the drawer and waited. I stood there for five minutes, but nothing happened. "I know you're here, darling. Open the drawer for me!" After a while, I gave up and went to bed and read while Stuart had a shower.

A few minutes later, we were both settled into bed and had turned out the lights. As we were nodding off to sleep, there was a loud crash in the bathroom.

"What was that?" said Stuart, jumping up.

"I hope it's what I think it is," I said, heading to the ensuite. I was simultaneously nervous and excited as I opened the bathroom door. As I flicked on the light, I was met with the sight of the drawer not only opened but entirely pulled out and sitting on the vanity.

"Thank you!" I whispered. "I'm sorry I can't hear you, but I know you're here. Don't worry, I'll tell your mum and dad you're all right."

"You're not going to believe this!" I told Stuart as I jumped back into bed. As I relayed the whole drawer-opening episode, he stared at me open-mouthed.

"Well, you're not going to believe *this*," he said. "When I went to have a shower, the drawer was open. I thought you left it like that, so I just shut it and thought nothing of it."

"No wonder the poor thing slammed the drawer on the vanity! She wanted to make sure I heard her and came in to investigate."

We were both stunned, but honoured to have had this visit. As I fell asleep, I knew what I had to do the next day. I needed to call Ivana and David to let them know their daughter was okay.

I awoke the following morning feeling awestruck, still unable to fully comprehend the previous night's events. I was torn between feeling elated and sad. I was happy to be able to provide some validation for Ivana and David, but sad that such a beautiful young girl was no longer with us. I was also humbled at being on the receiving end of yet more proof of life after death. I felt emotional at the thought of those who have died remaining so close to their loved ones, and grateful to be in a position to verify this for myself.

Despite my intention to contact Ivana and David the day after Sarah's visit, it took me three days to muster up the courage to call them. When I finally braced myself and dialed their number, David answered and I was momentarily thrown, unsure of how he would take the news of his daughter's visit. I ran through the whole story, from the first time I met Ivana, to the flashing lights, and finally the opening of the drawer. He listened quietly. I had no idea what he was thinking, and hoped that he believed what I was telling him.

Once the story was told, David thanked me, grateful to me for sharing my experience. But the revelation was bittersweet, because despite evidence of Sarah's continued survival, it just didn't compare to a reality where he is able to put his arms around her. I realised that proof that Sarah lives on in another dimension simply cannot compare to the joys of watching her blossom into a woman. I totally understood that it could never be enough.

Later that evening, Ivana called, and I relayed my story once again. I apologised that I couldn't forward a message, although I was sure Sarah had a lot she wanted to say. I explained that despite being clairvoyant and able to see spirits, I am not clairaudient, and on only a handful of occasions have I been able to hear spirits.

Ivana and I arranged to meet the following Wednesday to go to the local Spiritualist church and hopefully provide Sarah with the opportunity to get her message through.

Ivana and I met before the service and shared a heartfelt embrace. Despite this being only the second time we had met, we had already laid the foundations for what I had no doubt would be a lifelong friendship.

We sat side by side in the fluoro-lit room; the atmosphere was charged and I was happy to feel Sarah's presence. By the time we were halfway through the service, I was convinced Ivana would receive a message, and was overwhelmed by a sense of expectation as the medium walked to the front of the congregation.

It didn't take long for my excitement to dwindle, as after the first two readings it was obvious that the medium was firing off one cliché after another, with little convincing validation of the presence of spirits. I couldn't help but squirm as the medium crossed the room and all attention turned to me.

"I want to come to the lady in green," she said. "You're from the U.K., aren't you?"

"No." I shook my head.

"Well, not you as such, your family..." I continued to shake my head, smiling so as not to come across as too negative. The medium was refusing to take no for an answer. "Well, it goes way back. Your grandparents, perhaps? Or maybe even your great grandparents?..."

"My family is from Croatia," I said.

"Oh! I knew it was from around there somewhere!" She smiled unconvincingly. "Well, there is an old woman here offering you a tray of scones. Does that mean anything to you? Can you place an elderly woman who liked baking?"

I inwardly cringed and berated myself for wasting an entire evening to hear someone cold read the expectant congregation before her. I felt insulted and disappointed, particularly because I knew there were spirits like Sarah present who had important messages to relay. Just when I thought it couldn't get any worse, the medium threw another cliché my way before moving on to her next victim.

"Just think about it," she said. "It'll dawn on you who I'm talking about. She's leaving now and she's offering you a large bouquet of roses..." Ivana and I looked at each other, dangerously close to bursting into laughter. We were both thinking the same thing: "What a load of rubbish!"

Not wishing the entire evening to be wasted, we headed back up the hill to my place supposedly for a coffee but ended up cracking open a bottle of red wine. I showed Ivana the porcelain drawers that Sarah had opened a few nights earlier, and she smiled when she saw them.

"You know, Sarah would've absolutely loved those! They are exactly the sort of thing she would buy!"

I also showed her the statue of an angel I had bought the week before to commemorate Sarah and to acknowledge her visits to our home. The statue is of a lithe silver beauty, dressed in a long bronze dress. "That's my Sarah," smiled Ivana. "Tall, slim, long black hair, just like a model!" We smiled at each other, knowing that Sarah had somehow brought us together. We returned downstairs and sat by the fire, talking well into the night. From that evening onwards, we have become the closest of friends.

To this day, Sarah has continued to show herself to me as a brilliant light directly above her mother's head. It is as bright and intense as the day I first saw her, and continues to affirm the fact that she remains strongly connected to her family.

A few months after our first meeting, Ivana and I were sitting in the downstairs family room when Sarah decided to put in an appearance. Her spirit light was so vivid that I suggested we try to capture it on film, and the photographs we took that evening were amazing, to say the least.

Stuart grabbed the camera as Ivana cuddled Sarah's beloved dog Holly, and I muscled in beside her for good measure. We asked Sarah if she would please appear in our photo, and we were delighted to see her spirit light shining above her mother's head in the very first shot.

It is one thing to be told a loved one's spirit is present, but to have photographic evidence is another thing altogether.

This was such a convincing validation of Sarah's presence that we were all absolutely delighted. It confirmed in Ivana's mind that when I tell her that her daughter is around her, she is shining above her as brilliantly as the brightest star.

Chapter Eleven

Sister David

Another dear friend I made through my work was Sister David, as unlikely a friend as I ever could have imagined.

Sister David could best be described as a kindhearted larrikin (a playful rebel), her grey and white habit belying the vibrant character hiding underneath. At first glance she was typically what one would expect for an elderly nun, greying and slightly stooped, but when she opened her mouth all preconceptions went flying out the window.

I first met Sister David in the early 1990s as she was the designated chauffeur for St. Emilie's Convent. She frequently ferried nuns to and from their podiatry appointments, and I often saw her running errands around Kalamunda. She had a perpetual look of amusement on her face, and what struck me most was her cheeky sense of humour. Much to the mortification of her fellow Catholic sisters, her standard reply to the ubiquitous "How are you?" was "Nearly dead, thank God!" When I eventually came to ask her why she said this, she replied that she was just making sure that whoever was enquiring after her well-being was actually paying attention. "More often than not, they're not even listening!" she laughed.

Over the years I developed a great affection for Sister David, who was usually accompanied by the somewhat more sedate Sister Agnes. Sister Agnes was the antithesis of her vivacious sidekick, counterbalancing her friend's cheekiness with her gentle reserve. Since Sister Agnes attended my clinic every four weeks, the two nuns became regular fixtures in my life over the course of fifteen years. They shared the joy of my wedding and the arrival of my children, being amongst the first visitors to welcome Eloise when I first became a mother. They supported me through both heartbreaks and celebrations, and were an unwavering presence.

One particularly fond memory is from 2007, soon after our daughter Claire broke her arm. Claire had just been released from hospital, after requiring surgery to realign her fractured ulna. I was walking around the shopping complex in Kalamunda trying to find a suitable get well gift when I ran into Sister David and told her about Claire's accident. She was visibly saddened by the news, and I could see her mind ticking over as she spoke to me. "Poor love," she said. "Now what can we do to cheer her up?"

The answer arrived the following day, when my receptionist called me from the clinic. She told me Sister David had called to offer Claire a gift, and *hoped I wouldn't have a*

Sister Agnes and Sister David (with babe in arms) were amongst the first visitors to come and greet our new arrival, Eloise. The two nuns played a pivotal role in my life for many years, offering love and support through good times and bad.

problem with it. She was offering the use of a large brass bell, to ensure the little patient's every whim was catered to during her recovery. I couldn't help but laugh, but the thought of a clanging school bell commanding my attention was more than I could bear. We compromised by allowing Claire a smaller bell instead, and every time it rang I was reminded of my funny, caring friend.

It was some time in the following year that Sister Agnes could no longer make the trip to my clinic; she was becoming frail and required a visiting podiatrist to make a domiciliary visit to the convent instead. As such, I lost touch with my favourite sisters for a few months and had no idea that Sister David had become gravely ill. By the time I discovered she had pancreatic cancer, she was in palliative care at Kalamunda Hospital.

I was devastated by the news, and decided to cancel my patients for the rest of the afternoon and go spend some time with her. I called the palliative care ward to check on visiting times, and was shattered when the nurse told me not to bother.

"Probably best if you don't come," she said. "Sister won't have any idea that you're here anyway." She fobbed me off, and I was left feeling helpless and unsure of what I should do. I couldn't help thinking that this time Sister David really was "nearly dead, thank God," and wondered at the irony of her favourite comment.

Later that evening, just as I resolved to hold my ground and go to the hospital the following day, I saw Sister David grinning at me from the darkness. She was radiant and young, and she was posing as the Statue of Liberty, her right arm held aloft. "I'm freeeeee!" she cried, as clearly as though she was shouting in my ear. I burst into tears, knowing without a doubt that my old friend had passed away. But part of me was rejoicing with her, as she was no doubt completely relishing the next phase of her journey.

I didn't see Sister David's spirit again, but I wonder if she is one of the filmy figures who visit my waiting room from time to time. Nearly two years after her death, I suspected this might be the case as one of my patients walked in for her appointment. Alison is a sensitive soul who confided in me at one of her earlier appointments that from time to time she sees spirits.

"You do realise there's a nun in your backyard, don't you?" she laughed. I was momentarily confused, unsure as to whether she was referring to a living person or a spirit. Alison obviously picked up on my puzzled expression as she went on to tell me she often saw the spirit of a nun whilst sitting in my waiting room.

It is wonderful to think that Sister David still visits me, and receiving confirmation from a third party who knows nothing about my relationship with her validates her presence all the more. And I can't help but think that when my time comes and I am "nearly dead, thank God," Sister David may very well be in the welcoming party waiting on the other side.

Betty

As time went on, I found that I was connecting with my patients on more than just a professional level. I was frequently in tune with the spirit presences around them. I was also honoured with post-death visits, particularly from those patients who were aware of my clairvoyant abilities in the years prior to their deaths. It made me wonder if my patients had been planning to drop by all along, or whether it had occurred to them only after they had died. Did they suddenly think, *Hey! I know who'll be able to see me!*

Either way, I have been privileged to be on the receiving end of many visits, the most recent of which took things to a new and thrilling level.

Betty had been my patient for around ten years, during which time we saw each other every couple of months. She was a trained physiotherapist and mother of three. We found we had a lot in common despite our forty-year age gap.

I was particularly in awe of Betty's achievements as a physiotherapist. She carved out a career for herself at a time when it was the norm to be a stay-at-home mother. Her achievements were even more impressive when one considers that she was a single mother, after divorcing her husband when her children were still young.

At eighty years of age, Betty seemed agile and healthy, so her sudden fatal heart attack came as a shock. When her daughter Alison called to tell me the news, she was still trying to come to terms with the fact that her vibrant mother had been happily enjoying a family dinner one moment, and lying on the floor the next.

Alison and her family had just spent a happy weekend with Betty, and being able to share in her mother's precious final days is something for which she is grateful.

When Alison came to see me two days after her mother's death, we talked about Betty's final moments. She told me that when she called for an ambulance she was just going through the motions, as she had no doubt that her mother had already died.

She knew there was no hope of saving her mother because she could see Betty's spirit up in the corner of the room, looking down at her body.

"I know it sounds crazy," said Alison. "But she really was up there!"

I assured her it didn't sound crazy at all, as I had experienced similar things myself. Alison wanted to know more, but our conversation was disrupted by a bright flashing light just above Alison's shoulder.

"Well, there you go," I said. "That's all the confirmation I need. Your mum is definitely keeping an eye on you!"

"Can you please tell her I love her?" asked Alison, becoming teary.

"No need," I told her. "You just did."

Two days later I was spending a quiet day at home when I felt a spirit around me, and decided to try to tune in.

I went downstairs and lay on the lounge, allowing myself to fall into the semi-trance state in which I am most receptive. It didn't take long before the room began to buzz with energy, and shortly after, the fuzziness was pierced by a beautiful bright light just past my feet.

I was, of course, expecting Betty, but I wanted to validate her presence rather than just assume it was her.

Since I was still working on developing my clairaudience, I decided to try to establish an alternate mode of communication that would allow Betty to identify herself.

"Betty! Is that you?"

Flash!

Good! I thought, but it wasn't good enough.

"Betty," I said, "if it's you, can you please touch my leg?"

Almost immediately I felt a firm pressure on my left leg, almost like a reassuring pat just above my knee.

I was beginning to feel excited, but tried to remain in a relaxed and receptive state so I wouldn't sabotage the communication.

"Can you touch my head now?"

Again, mere seconds after I'd asked the question, I felt a gentle tapping sensation right on the top of my head.

"Again?" I asked.

Tap, tap, tap!

By now I was getting really excited and decided to put any lingering fears aside and take things one step further.

"Can you show me how you died?"

The sensation that overtook me was sudden and intense. My chest was suddenly crushed by an incredible feeling of pressure, together with a steadily mounting tightness. I wasn't sure if my acute breathlessness came as part of the demonstration or whether it was a result of my fear.

"Okay, that's enough now!" I said, and the sensations stopped immediately.

It's hard to reconcile the two extremes of emotion I was feeling. Although it was frightening to be so wholly experiencing the symptoms of a fatal heart attack, I was thrilled to know Betty was paying me a visit. I was also happy to be experiencing such a concrete manifestation of a spirit presence, as it reinforced that my abilities were developing beyond my limited clairvoyance.

Bolstered by the realisation that I was not having a real heart attack and the spirit was almost undoubtedly Betty, I decided to ask her how she died one more time, just to be sure.

And as before, the crushing sensation descended immediately. The tightness in my chest became progressively more intense, like a fierce and endless contraction. After a few seconds I asked her to stop and just like that, it did. Heart attack over!

Buoyed by my successful communication (especially since I knew it was Betty), I dashed upstairs in search of my camera, eager for that last little piece of proof.

"Okay, Betty," I said, coming back downstairs. "After this I'm going to stop harassing you! Could you please shine your spirit light for me just one more time? I'd really love you to appear in my photo!"

I don't think I have met as compliant a spirit before or since, as with one quick snap Betty was there, as a bright luminous orb shining in my photo! Each of my requests had been responded to. She was as eager a communicator from the spirit world as she had been in life.

Betty proved to me that she was present and reinforced the fact that spirit communication is to be celebrated rather than feared. My interaction with Betty took my abilities to the next level. Now I had the ability to see spirits and interact with them on a physical level. And rather than being frightened, the very thought of it thrilled me!

The Artist in the Hallway

Being in private practice for so many years, it is easy to get bored and disillusioned with the day-to-day workload of a podiatrist. Just when I think I could not possibly face another ingrown toenail or heel spur, someone walks through the door to revive my flagging enthusiasm. One of the great things about my job is that I have the opportunity to meet people from all walks of life, and connect with them on a one-on-one basis. Often they are people whom I would otherwise have never met, and I remind myself that I am in a privileged position to meet so many new and interesting people.

When Dan Gullotti first walked through my door, he exuded warmth and a sense of *joie de vivre.* With his greying hair and crinkly-eyed smile, he was the classic Italian gentleman. For the ten years that I knew him, we saw each other no more than three or four times a year, yet he always greeted me with an enthusiastic embrace and the customary two kisses.

He was a highly accomplished artist and was the art master at a prestigious college in Australia for twenty-two years. His paintings hang in the National Gallery of Australia, yet his humility belied his artistic brilliance, and no one would ever have imagined they were in the company of a highly lauded artist.

It was several years into our friendship before I visited Dan's studio, and when I did, I was entranced by the paintings before me. I was so taken with Dan's beautiful paintings that I decided to buy two, and my children had the privilege of choosing their favourites. Since they were an expensive luxury, I paid them off over the course of several years, dropping off a hundred dollars here and there whenever I had extra money.

Dan kept insisting that I take the paintings immediately, but I told him I would rather wait until they were paid for, and as such, almost four years had passed by the time I took them home. And by then, Dan had died.

It was a bittersweet moment as I finally took possession of my precious paintings. As Dan's wife, Carlotta, handed me the bubble-wrapped treasures, I couldn't help but wish that I had taken the paintings earlier, as I had missed out on the joy of accepting them from Dan himself. Carlotta and I were both emotional, and as we stood together in Dan's studio, his energy was palpable around us.

I took the paintings home and, after trying out several potential places to display them, settled on hanging them in our entry hall. They are poignant and beautiful, and very few people come to our home without commenting on our wonderful artwork.

It was some months before I noticed him for the first time, and from then on he made his presence known almost every day. Whenever I walked out of my bedroom I saw him, a figure standing at the end of the hallway, like a silent sentinel keeping watch over his charges.

I had no idea it was Dan, and I was frustrated that someone was reaching out to me and I didn't know what they wanted. All I saw was a pale white figure of medium build and average height. I knew he was male, but I just couldn't place him.

One night as I came out of the bathroom and went down the hall, he was right there, standing no more than an arm's length away. For a split second I saw him in colour.

"I see you!" I said out loud. "You're wearing jeans and a white T-shirt!" But his face still escaped me, so in frustration I sought out the help of my friend Giulia.

"There's someone standing in my hallway and it's driving me crazy. I can't work out who it is!"

I asked Giulia if she could come over, as I interpreted the spirit's insistence as him needing to get a message across; I was worried that he needed help. Giulia was pensive for a moment, and it didn't take long before she tuned in to my spirit friend in the hallway.

"Barbie," she said, "the paintings in your hallway…is the artist dead?"

As soon as she asked me, I got goose bumps, my fool-proof sign that what I'm hearing is the truth. The spirit was, of course, my good friend Dan Gullotti.

"Giulia! You're right!" I said, feeling more than a little foolish at not having worked it out for myself. "Do you know what he wants?"

"He's happy," she told me. "He just wants to say good-bye." I was suddenly flushed with happiness as I realised Dan was with me when I took possession of the paintings after all. When I got off the phone I rushed into the hallway, and there he was. With his distinct build and posture, I was now astounded that I hadn't placed him right away. I saw him for only a few seconds, just long enough for him to flash a brilliant light at me from his chest, and then he was gone. I stared at my paintings and fell in love with them anew; no artwork could ever be so precious.

I still think of Dan often and am grateful for my beautiful paintings. But even more so, I am grateful to my old friend for showing me once again that life is more amazing than we can ever truly fathom. He has reminded me that true friendship, like love, is not hindered by death. It continues to thrive and nurture us from the hallways of another dimension.

Chapter Twelve

Meeting Max

Some of the bubbliest people I know are those who have endured the greatest tragedies. It seems as though the intensity of their experiences has somehow enriched them, and their triumph over heartbreak is an inspiration to us all.

I have often wondered whether these people are perhaps wise old souls who have chosen their painful paths for the purpose of spiritual growth. Perhaps they have made a pre-incarnation contract with their loved ones and they travel their painful road together in order to grow. Spiritual growth stems from experiencing every extreme of emotion, and it is the ways in which we rise above the blows of the most painful experiences that ultimately allow us to grow.

I first met Charmaine at my son's kindergarten, as her daughter Lilli was Daniel's classmate. It took some weeks before we actually spoke to each other, as we both seemed to be perpetually rushing, trying to cram in jobs and house-work in between the twice-daily school runs.

We often exchanged smiles and quick hellos, but it was some weeks into our acquaintance before we found our-selves with an opportunity to actually talk.

When I told Charmaine that I was the local podiatrist, she stared at me wide-eyed and started laughing.

"That is so weird! I was just telling my brother that I was considering studying podiatry! I'm soooooo over nursing!"

"Well, I'm soooooo over podiatry!"

We spoke to each other more and more often, and as the weeks went by I discovered the reason for Charmaine ditch-ing her nursing career. Five years earlier she had lost her seven-year-old son Max, after nursing him through a long, drawn-out battle with cancer. There was just no way she could go back.

I found Charmaine inspiring on so many levels. Max's death was a catalyst for Charmaine to leave a toxic, unhappy marriage, as she felt she owed it to Max to settle for nothing but the best for herself and her children.

She singlehandedly maintained her three-acre property, and thought little of cutting down trees, clearing gutters, and rendering vast expanses of ugly brickwork! She was a tiler, a painter, and a tinkerer; there was nothing she couldn't put her hand to.

To say I was impressed by Charmaine's renovating abili-ties would be a gross understatement; I was well and truly blown away. Her days were a constant stream of productivity and there was much to show for her efforts. Yet as impressed

*Gorgeous Max: Such a sweet little
soul. Although we didn't know each
other whilst Max was alive, I had
the privilege of meeting Max six
years after his passing. A cheeky
car enthusiast, Max's antics often
bring a smile to my face.*

as I was by her skills and abilities, it was her strength of heart
that impressed me the most.

I had a sense of Max in Charmaine's house straight away,
from the first day we sat together in her lounge room. Max
had passed away in that very room, yet the energy was
vibrant rather than sad, as though it was the scene of his
release.

When I looked at Charmaine I saw a bright flashing light
just above and a little behind her, and as we spoke about Max
it became more intense.

Charmaine told me she had no doubt that Max called in often, and relayed to me an experience she'd had only a couple of weeks earlier. Because Max had been a devoted car buff, many of his signs revolved around the family car.

One night as Charmaine was about to go to bed, she noticed that the carport light was on. Having retrieved something from the car an hour earlier, she suspected she had forgotten to turn it off and went outside to do so. She was met by the sight of all four car doors open, each at exactly the same angle. Since Lilli and her son Harry had long been in bed, she knew they couldn't have opened them. She also knew the open doors could not have been the work of a potential car thief, as there was no way an intruder could venture up her long, secluded driveway without alerting the attention of her dog Tyson.

Charmaine and I stood in the driveway as she relayed her story almost as an afterthought as I was about to go. At this point things began to get really strange.

We said our goodbyes and just as I was about to get into my car, the car doors locked. My first thought was that the central locking was playing up, so we shrugged it off and I unlocked the car. I went to open the door again and *click!* it locked once again.

"I'm starting to get the impression that Max doesn't want me to leave!" I said.

The same thing happened three times before I was able to get into my car and go.

"I told you he liked cars!" Charmaine called out as I drove off.

As I drove towards town, I was excited but cautious, knowing that it was possible for central locking devices to malfunction from time to time. Although I wanted to believe it was Max giving us a sign, I didn't want us to be reading into a perfectly logical happening; I was worried we may have been deluding ourselves.

"Maxy," I said out loud. "Are you still here? If you are, can you please lock my doors again?"

Almost instantaneously there was a loud *click* as all four car doors locked.

"Max!" I said. "Thank you! And thanks for not wanting me to leave your house, but I promise to go back again very soon."

Hoping for just one more validation, I had one final request.

"Hey Maxy, do you think I should buy your mum a special book to remember today by? I've only got five minutes before I have to pick up the kids, but if you could help me maybe I could quickly run into Ambrosium and get her that book I was telling her about…I know you've done so much today already, but how about just one more thing? Would you help me?"

I wasn't surprised when I pulled up outside the New Age bookstore and there was an empty parking bay right outside the front door. Nor was I surprised when I made a beeline for the book I wanted (*Journey of Souls* by Michael Newton) sitting right before my eyes on the bookshelf waiting for me.

"Thanks, sweetie!" I said as I jumped back in the car, and headed off to pick up the children and give Charmaine her book.

Max's Birthday

For those who have lost loved ones, birthdays and anniversaries can be particularly painful, as it is natural to wish that those who've passed away were here to share them with us. As painful as they may feel, these times should in fact be embraced, as it then that spirits draw close to their loved ones, radiating their comfort and love.

With what would've been Max's thirteenth birthday looming, Charmaine was hoping to keep the day low-key, not sure how she would cope with the emotions that would no doubt be dredged up. Her fifteen-year-old son Harry, however, had a different idea altogether, and refused to allow the day to pass without due celebration.

"So what are we doing for Max's thirteenth?" he asked repeatedly. "We've gotta do something!"

Charmaine was torn between wanting to let the day pass quietly and acquiescing to Harry's wishes, especially since a nagging inner voice told her that celebrating Max's birthday was the right thing to do. Regardless, putting the plan into action was difficult, so at Harry's urging I decided to intervene.

"How about we have a little party?" I asked Charmaine. "Just you, Harry, and Lilli and me and the kids?"

"Yeah," interrupted Harry, "that'd be awesome!"

Charmaine agreed as much for Harry and Lilli's sake as Max's, knowing that they all deserved to commemorate this very special day. So the plan was set; we would meet straight after school on Max's birthday, determined to give a most special day the attention it deserved.

The weather couldn't have been more perfect; it was balmy with the hint of a breeze, just enough to carry away the helium balloons we were planning to release at our celebration. Each of us had written Max a birthday message on small red paper hearts, which we had slipped inside the balloons before they were inflated.

It was particularly poignant that, when asked to select a balloon for the brother she had never met, five-year-old Lilli chose the very same type of balloon Max had floating in his room the week before he died. It was a bright yellow smiley face and Max had absolutely loved it.

We made an appropriately festive birthday cake oozing with melted chocolate bars, strawberries, and cream in between layers of hazelnut meringue. There was champagne for the mothers and lemonade for the kids. The scene was set and we were ready to party!

Of course I had no doubt that Max would be in attendance. Almost as soon as we entered the house, I saw his spirit light flashing. It was bright and exuberant and as excited as we were.

I assembled the children around Tyson the dog, and asked Max if he would also like to be in our photo. My request was rewarded with a massive glowing orb positioned just above the children, fulfilling Max's role as star of the show.

As we sang "Happy Birthday," the energy around us heightened, and as the numerous photos from the day attest, we were all grinning like idiots. Our voices grew ever louder as we sang, and on the final *hip, hip, hooooooraaaaaaaaaaaay!* we released our cluster of multicoloured balloons, and whooped as they made their escape toward the heavens.

Like a pack of wild animals, we laughed as we ran down the length of the property, scrambling through rockery and bushes as we traced the path of the balloons. We ran right down to the bottom fence line until Max's balloons were the tiniest of specks on the horizon, rising ever upward.

"Happy birthday, Maaaaaaaaax!!!" we screeched at the tops of our voices, then promptly looked at each other and began to laugh. Even poor Harry, who had suffered a nasty graze in the mad scramble, couldn't help laughing, such was the joyousness of the moment.

When we went back indoors to continue our celebration, Max had beaten us to it. As we walked into the lounge room, his spirit light was waiting, flashing excitedly as we filed into the room. I even managed to capture an orb photo when he flashed at me from the sofa, which amused me as it seemed Max was chilling after the frantic excitement of the balloon run.

Later, as Charmaine and I sat down for a quiet glass of champagne, Max drew right in close to his mother.

"One last pic before we call it a night?" I asked.

"Sure," smiled Charmaine.

And in that moment as I pressed down on the button, Max shone brilliantly and beautifully, especially for his mother.

L–R: Charmaine, Harry, Lilli, Claire, and Eloise prepare to launch celebratory balloons for Max's thirteenth birthday. We each wrote a special message for Max, which we placed in the balloons beforehand.

As I showed Charmaine the photo, she was thrilled but not surprised.

"Oh, he's here all right," she said. "Never doubted it for a moment!"

When I think back to Max's thirteenth birthday, the overwhelming emotion I feel is joy. It's hard to explain the connection I felt with Max on that day, but I felt closer to him than one normally would when attending a teenage friend's birthday party. Which leads me to wonder, what exactly is it that we gain when we pass over? A greater sense of connectedness to each other? An increase in clarity? An abundance of unconditional love? I feel that it's all three, amongst myriad other gifts that we as mortals can't even begin to understand.

What I do know is that every spirit I have connected with has left me feeling loved, humbled, and happy, as I suspect they have been let in on a few secrets that are still beyond our understanding. It is at times like these that I am very grateful for my gift.

Of course for Charmaine, and indeed everyone who has lost a loved one, birthdays will forever be bittersweet. But if, like Charmaine, the bereaved can glean the positives out of the life that has been lost, and allow happy memories and love to penetrate the grief, then the pain can be balanced with a healthy dose of joyfulness.

Firefly

My children have been raised to embrace the existence of spirits, and I have tried to nurture the innate sensitivities that I believe all children are born with. On the occasions when they tell me they have seen spirits, I always react positively, and tell them they are lucky to be in tune with the other side.

Similarly, I have never hidden my own experiences from the children, as I firmly believe that it's the unknown that fosters fear. It was fear that fuelled the negative experiences of my childhood, and I would hate for them to unwittingly expose themselves to a similar situation. They accept that spirits are a normal inclusion in the tapestry of life, and have come to appreciate that spirits happily coexist around us.

All three of them have been eager participants in sessions of orb photography, and they have come to consider spirit presences to be a positive rather than a frightening aspect of life. On the occasions when we have encountered ghosts, I have tried to maintain a similar positivity, despite sometimes feeling fearful myself.

My husband, Stuart, is grounded and a realist, but has always been open to the possibility of life on the other side. He has known of my paranormal experiences since our first meeting in 1994, and although he has never doubted their authenticity, he has often expressed a desire for some proof of his own. The chain of events that saw this desire come to fruition began on a low-key Friday afternoon.

Stuart was on shift at the fire station when the call came through. In a matter of minutes the pump and light tanker were belting down the main highway, bound for a grass fire in a neighbouring suburb.

Upon the crew's arrival, the source of the fire was immediately apparent. A shallow pit was piled with smouldering logs, which had in turn set fire to the long, dry grass along the adjacent fence lines.

Being a hot, windy afternoon, the fire crew ensured that the threatening flames were contained quickly, and it was not long before the reserve was blanketed in a layer of grey-white smoke. Stuart was spraying water into the pit as he methodically removed the logs one by one, ensuring the fire was fully extinguished.

He had almost cleared the last of the logs when he tossed a smoking bundle towards the growing pile. It fell to the ground with a thud, but it sounded different than the countless logs that had preceded it. Looking over to where it had landed, he could barely comprehend the sight before him. A woman's torso, limbless and charred, lay on the gravel track before him.

The police were summoned to what was obviously a murder scene; the area was cordoned off and secured. Once statements were taken and the formalities completed, the fire crew returned to the station and booked off shift. I knew something was wrong when Stuart came home in the early afternoon, well before his usual knock-off time.

He told me that he had discovered a murder victim. It was obvious that he was deeply shaken; the afternoon suddenly felt surreal.

Once the shock subsided, Stuart was swamped by myriad emotions, predominantly guilt. He berated himself for throwing the woman, having mistaken her for a burning log. Firefighters are committed to treating people with respect and dignity, regardless of their condition, and Stuart felt as though he had failed to uphold this doctrine. No amount of reassurance could ease his remorse, as he couldn't see past the way he had treated the woman's remains. It was of little comfort that the police apprehended the perpetrator later that evening, largely due to the retrieval of her body and the discovery of incriminating forensic evidence.

Deciding that distraction and the support of his fellow firefighters would help him come to terms with the day's events, Stuart headed off to a social club gathering after dinner. Alone with our three children, I settled them into bed and prepared for an early night. I felt the murdered woman's presence and was uneasy as I got into bed with my book. Confirmation came a few minutes later when I heard my young son's train set buzz into life. I rushed into his bedroom to turn it off before he woke up, all the while wondering if she was watching me. I returned to bed anxiously, waiting for another sign.

I didn't have to wait long; again she chose one of the children's toys, this time the toy guitar. The tinny notes of "Cock a Doodle Do!" rang through the house as I hunted through baskets full of toys, straining to hear exactly where the music was coming from. I eventually found the guitar downstairs inside the coffee table, and firmly switched it off. I was shaken but didn't feel threatened; I knew she was desperate for my attention. Returning to the bedroom, I briefly glimpsed her sitting on Stuart's side of the bed, so I decided to continue my reading elsewhere until he returned home.

Contrary to Stu's self-condemnation, I felt certain that the woman was grateful to him for finding her. In the days that followed, I often saw her sitting on our bed, always on Stuart's side. I was convinced she was offering comfort. I reminded Stu that a less thorough firefighter would have simply blasted water at the burning logs rather than removing the contents of the pit, and consequently would have failed to discover the body that lay hidden within. I pointed out that if it wasn't for him, the killer would possibly still be at large. But it was of little comfort and he struggled, guilt-ridden and traumatised, for countless sleepless weeks.

Then one night as he was preparing to come to bed, he saw her for himself. He came into our bedroom, ashen; the hairs were raised on the back of his neck.

"I just got my wish and I don't think I like it," he said, as he had often expressed a desire to see a ghost. I congratulated him on his first sighting, and asked him what he had seen. He described her exactly as I had seen her: small and slender, her body shape defined by dense, inky blackness. He saw her for only a few seconds as she disappeared down our hallway.

If Stuart had any doubts about what he saw, they were dispelled in the early hours of the following morning when our two-year-old woke up in the middle of the night screaming. We rushed into Daniel's bedroom to ask him what was wrong, as he rarely woke during the night.

Sobbing, he told us he "got scared by the lady…the black lady next to the bed…with no ears." We soothed our crying boy and, despite our initial pangs of uneasiness, felt sure our visitor posed no threat and was just keeping an eye on us.

Once she made her presence felt, and Stuart began to feel better, we saw no sign of her for almost two years. She returned the night before Stuart was due to give evidence at her murder trial, and was almost unrecognisable. She stood at the foot of our bed, no longer an ominous dark figure, but a radiant young woman.

She was grinning at me; I saw her for only a split second, and then she was gone. I questioned whether it was her at all until the following morning when I saw her face in the newspaper, as beautiful as she had appeared the night before.

The trial concluded a fortnight later, her killer sentenced to life imprisonment. A chapter closed and a new lightness washed over our household. We were never to see her again, but feel she is now at peace and that justice has been done.

Chapter Thirteen

Albany

A few weeks later we decided to take off to Albany, as Stuart was keen to try his luck in one of the local fishing tournaments. Albany is the site of the first settlement in Western Australia, and is rich in folklore and history. It is reputed to be one of the most haunted places in the state, and there is no shortage of potentially haunted locations to explore.

As it turned out, we didn't need to seek out any ghosts; they found us without any effort on our part whatsoever!

We checked into our holiday accommodation late on a Thursday afternoon. It was almost dark and drizzling, and the temperature was rapidly plummeting to its icy overnight low.

Despite my clairvoyant visions remaining somewhat hazy, my sensitivity to the presence of spirits was becoming progressively more honed. So when I walked into the holiday apartment, it was immediately apparent that there was someone there already.

I busied myself with the necessary chores of bathing the children and preparing dinner, whilst Stuart unloaded the car. It was not until much later that I began to tune in to the presence, once the children were quietly settled into bed.

As Stuart and I relaxed and watched some late-night television, I suddenly noticed a short figure standing across the room observing us. I said a mental *hi*, as is my usual practice, and headed off to bed shortly after, exhausted after a long day spent driving from Perth. I had no doubt that someone was there, but I was too tired to give it much thought.

The following morning, Stuart headed off for some pre-competition fishing practice, and I was alone with the children. Before heading out to explore Albany, I decided to get a few chores out of the way, and told the children to play for the hour or so until we left. Eloise and Daniel played in the lounge area, whilst Claire went to the children's bedroom to read. It was barely five minutes later when Claire came in to the lounge to join her siblings.

"Had enough of reading already?" I joked. "It mustn't be a very good book!" Claire just looked at me and didn't say a word. It wasn't until a few hours later that I discovered the reason she didn't want to remain in the bedroom alone.

We headed off shortly after, and enjoyed a day of exploring the sights of Albany. We began with a visit to the Brig Amity, a replica of the sailing vessel that brought the first white settlers from Sydney in 1826. The afternoon was spent at the old Albany gaol, yet despite its obvious eeriness there wasn't a ghost to be seen, and I couldn't help feeling just a little disappointed.

By the time we returned to the apartment in the afternoon, we were cold and tired and looked forward to relaxing
by the fire. The children went to put their things in their bedroom, and seconds later I heard Eloise calling me.

"Mum! I think you should come and see this!"

I rushed into the bedroom and the children showed me
a small mound of dirt on the upper bunk, neatly piled on
top of the bedclothes. My first thought was that one of the
children had gotten onto the bed with their sandy shoes, but
I quickly remembered their shoes were all lined up outside
the front door. I then reasoned that there must have been a
hole in the ceiling, and climbed onto the bunk bed to exam-
ine the plaster directly above it. I tapped the ceiling with my
fingertips…nothing. I began to bang on it more forcefully,
but not a drop of dirt fell; it was perfectly intact. I swept up
the mess and tried to dismiss it, but suspected the young boy
I glimpsed the night before was playing tricks on us.

It was little more than fifteen minutes later when Claire
came running out of the bedroom and told me another pile
of sand had mysteriously appeared on the bed. Again it was
on the same upper bunk, but this time farther towards the
foot of the bed. "Mum, I think it was the boy!" she said. "The
one I saw in the bedroom this morning!"

"Maybe he just wants to play," I said, not wanting to
frighten her. But I felt decidedly uneasy, and couldn't help
feeling the young ghost was not happy with us being there.
The mound of dirt reappeared four times throughout the
course of the afternoon, and we found each one mere minutes after the preceding pile was swept away.

I imagine that the young ghost boy tired of the dirt game and proceeded to raise the bar in his attention-seeking endeavours.

By now it was almost dinnertime, and I busied myself in the kitchen whilst the children watched television in the adjacent lounge area. I was walking past the cooker when there was a sudden *whoooosh!* and flames flew from the gaps around the poorly sealed oven door. My jeans were singed, and I screamed as the flames leapt at my legs. I was stunned, especially since the gas oven wasn't turned on at the time. The whole episode was over in a matter of seconds, but I was still shaken when Stuart returned half an hour later.

I decided to speak to the owner, and asked her whether there had been any complaints about the oven being faulty. She told me it was almost new, and no one else had mentioned any problems with it. She assured me she would send a technician to our unit to check it. I also enquired as to any problems with the ceiling; I was loath to come straight out and tell her that I thought the unit was haunted. But when I mentioned piles of sand on the bed, there was a glimmer of recognition, and I could tell that this was not the first time someone had complained about it.

"Ah…yes, the sand…that does happen from time to time. I'll get the tech to check the ceiling for you too."

As I turned to leave, she called out to me, "In the meantime, I can move you to unit seven if you like." Our eyes met and in that instant I was convinced that she knew the unit was haunted. "If you can be bothered moving your stuff, you're welcome to it."

"Thanks," I smiled. "I think we'll take you up on that!"

We moved our belongings to the new apartment in record time, and Stuart and I rewarded ourselves with a celebratory drink. Not only was the new unit ghost-free, it was also much bigger, with not a mound of dirt to be seen.

When we checked out a few days later, I wasn't surprised when the owner told me that the gas oven was thoroughly checked and deemed to be in perfect working order. The ceiling was similarly fault-free.

I noticed another family checking into the haunted apartment as we left, and was tempted to say something. I trust that their stay there was less eventful than our own, and hoped that the ghost boy was just feeding off my family's psychic energy. Perhaps he was trying to get a message across, other than the obvious one of "Get out!" Either way, I have not been brave enough to find out, and made sure we were booked into different accommodations when we returned to Albany two years later.

The Apartment

We began renovating our house in April 2009, and when it became uninhabitable, we temporarily moved to Stuart's grandparents' apartment in South Perth. It had been nine years since Gran had passed away, and Grandad had moved to a convalescent home, as he was too old and unwell to continue living alone. Their apartment on the South Perth foreshore had been empty for months, so when my mother-in-law suggested we relocate there for the duration of the renovations, we gratefully accepted.

Gran and Grandad first moved into their apartment in 1977, in what is undoubtedly one of the most desirable stretches of real estate in Perth. Directly opposite the city, the skyline juts just beyond the sparkling Swan River, which is dotted with ferries and pleasure craft. The foreshore buzzes with cyclists and pedestrians, creating a holiday atmosphere that we soon grew to love.

We moved into the apartment late on a Thursday afternoon, and as night fell the skyline lit up in a twinkling display of colour. It felt as though we could reach across the river and touch the buildings beyond, and I didn't tire of the view for the duration of our five-month stay.

I spent my first night there alone with the children, as Stuart was on night shift and wouldn't be joining us until the morning. I felt slightly apprehensive as I showered before bed, as I remembered that Gran was in the shower when she suffered her fatal stroke. Knowing how much she loved her home, I expected to sense her presence, and felt a little uneasy as I settled into her and Grandad's bed. I also couldn't help thinking that should Grandad die whilst we were staying there, he would waste no time returning to his much-loved home. With these thoughts in the forefront of my mind I had a fitful night's rest, on edge and expectant as I drifted in and out of sleep.

As the days went by, I definitely felt Gran around us, and I knew she would be delighted to have her great grandchildren injecting new life into her home. It was, however, two weeks until the conviction that Gran was around took on more substance, and it began at six in the morning on Stuart's forty-first birthday.

We were woken by the sound of a motorcycle revving its engine, and were initially confused by the strange raspy sounds emanating from Grandad's study. When Stuart went in to investigate, he realised it was the motorcycle alarm clock, and our first thought was that Gran was wishing him a happy birthday. We then reasoned that perhaps the children were playing with the alarm clock the day before, and resolved to keep an open mind before jumping to conclusions.

A few nights later I walked into Gran and Grandad's bedroom and saw the bedside lamp glowing on my side of the bed. The lamp was off, but emanated an eerie orange glow that brightened as I moved closer. When I stepped away, the light faded, and continued to vary its intensity depending on where I was in the room. My first thought was that it was Gran, but I wondered if there might be a logical explanation.

When there continued to be electrical disturbances, including the washing machine breaking down and the fridge refusing to work, we called in an electrician and had the wiring checked. We also mentioned that we'd had numerous unexplained blackouts, and pointed out the bedside lamp, which continued to mysteriously glow. The electrician conducted a thorough check and concluded that there was nothing wrong with the apartment's electrics, and was at a loss to explain the misbehaving light.

Things became even stranger when my mother-in-law, Cate, dropped by after visiting Grandad at the convalescent home over seventy kilometres away in Mandurah. Grandad was getting progressively more feeble, and it was obvious that his time on earth was coming to an end. Cate smiled as she relayed how Grandad had insisted that he had come back to the apartment the night before, and was horrified to discover it had been overtaken by *natives running amok and having a party.* Since we had been partying regularly during our stay, I wondered if Grandad had perhaps astrally travelled to his beloved home of over thirty years to find it overrun by noisy miscreants. From then on we toned things down, just in case Grandad was somehow keeping watch from his twilight state in the astral plane!

On Mother's Day a few weeks later, we were woken with the news that Grandad had died. The lunch that followed was bittersweet, as we were glad that Grandad's suffering was over but saddened by his passing. Friends and family gathered on the balcony as we shared food and drinks whilst reminiscing and enjoying the view.

Our friends Ivana and Dave were the first to arrive. We stood looking at a photo of Grandad that hung in the dining room, framed together with his medals and logbook that commemorated his service in the Royal Australian Air Force during World War Two. Ivana commented on how handsome he was and pointed out his resemblance to Bing Crosby. The compliments didn't go unnoticed, and seconds later Ivana was convinced she felt Grandad stroking her hair.

"Barbie," she laughed, "it's Grandad!" As we continued looking at the photo, she alternately felt him either touching her shoulder or her hair, neither of which surprised us, as Grandad was always known for being quite the lady's man!

The following night Eloise called me into Grandad's study, where she had taken to sleeping on an inflatable mattress on the floor.

She told me she was seeing little flashing lights. I asked her what they looked like, to which she replied they were like tiny red and blue dots. I was at once transported back to my own childhood, and memories of my nightly visitors came flooding back in a heady nostalgic wave.

"Do you think it's Grandad?" she asked.

"I'd be surprised if it wasn't," I said as I kissed her goodnight. Eloise smiled as she rolled over and settled down to sleep.

The final indication of Grandad's presence happened on the morning of his funeral, as we were preparing to drive to the family church in Mandurah. The children and I were getting dressed whilst Stuart was in the dining room. From the corner of his eye Stuart noticed movement, and turned to see a stout figure walk out of Grandad's bedroom and onto the adjacent balcony. For the instant that he was visible, there was no mistaking that the apparition was that of Stuart's late grandfather.

After the funeral the apartment resumed normality; the electrics no longer malfunctioned and there were no more lights or visions. The bedside lamp behaved itself and we felt that both Gran and Grandad had continued on their journey, happy to see their much-loved apartment filled with laughter and love once more.

Albany Again

Despite choosing our early 1900s holiday home specifically for its Victorian charm, I was immediately struck by a sense of foreboding when we pulled into its driveway. Stonecliffe House is a sprawling six-bedroom house overlooking Princess Royal Harbour, and together with the miserable weather formed the perfect backdrop for a paranormal encounter. It had been two years since our first Albany holiday, when a ghostly little boy harassed us by repeatedly piling mounds of sand onto the children's beds. I reasoned that if hauntings can occur in the most modern and unassuming of holiday apartments, then we might as well stay in a beautiful (albeit eerie) old house and take our chances!

We arrived on a rain-grey Monday afternoon. We were dismayed to discover that, contrary to the welcome we were expecting (with the front door key waiting in the letterbox and fires blazing in at least a couple of the house's nine fireplaces), there was no key and the house was bathed in darkness. We called the caretaker and arranged for the key to be dropped off, all the while wondering whether booking the house for a week had been such a good idea. The children and I peered through the windows while we waited, and were both captivated and unsettled by its Victorian décor.

One room in particular filled me with unease, a small wallpapered bedroom that was barely big enough to accommodate its child-sized wrought-iron bed. It reminded me of a similar room in Woodbridge House (a historic homestead on the banks of the Swan River) where the dead would be laid

This photo of our family was taken at a restaurant during our stay at Stonecliffe House in Albany…a welcome escape!

in state in the days preceding their funeral. "Death rooms" were a common feature in well-to-do homes in the early 1900s, and I couldn't help suspecting that the small room in question was hiding such a history.

By midafternoon we were settled in, fires were lit, and bedrooms were chosen. I was relieved that none of the children had chosen the small, creepy room. I found myself struggling to decide which room Stuart and I would occupy, as none of the remaining bedrooms felt particularly welcoming. We eventually settled on the large master suite upstairs, mostly because it was interconnected with the bedroom Claire and Daniel would be sharing.

Shortly before five o'clock, my sister, Vlasta, and brother-in-law, Michael, arrived. Their teenage son Alex had also come along, and they were all suitably impressed by Stonecliffe's grandeur. Predictably they also found it creepy, particularly since it was dusk and there was a storm threatening just off the coast.

We busied ourselves with dinner preparations, and as we played music and enjoyed a pre-dinner drink, the atmosphere lightened. We played board games by the fire after dinner, and although I was seeing numerous bright flashes, they were no more prevalent than elsewhere. I occasionally felt as though someone was touching my hair, but put it down to a mild case of paranoia.

It was well after midnight by the time we retired to our bedrooms. I went to check the front door and found it unlocked, and I was surprised that my security-conscious husband had been so remiss.

"Lucky I checked the door," I said. "We could've just spent the whole night with the front door open." Stuart assured me he had checked the door just minutes ago, going so far as to give it a good shake to ensure it was locked. My first thought was *Okay, here we go. I wonder what's next...*

After checking on the children, I walked back through the sitting room, and my heart skipped a beat as the overhead light began to flicker on and off. I tried to dismiss it as being caused by the typically faulty wiring of an old home, but couldn't shake the feeling that it was something more.

The night that followed was restless to say the least. Despite happily joining in with board games for several hours in the evening, Claire suddenly began to feel unwell upon lying down. She started to shake uncontrollably and was ill several times throughout the night. Having all eaten the same food, I did not think it was a case of food poisoning, and her temperature was normal. She looked pale and scared. "Did you get a fright?" I asked her. "Has something upset you?"

"I don't know what it is," she said. "I just started to feel weird as soon as I lay in that bed…" Stuart and I bundled her in between us, but it was some time (and several trips to the bathroom) before her shaking stopped and she dropped off to sleep.

The following morning Vlasta and Michael told us they'd had a strange experience as they got into bed, as a sudden cloying stench entered their bedroom. The experience lasted about fifteen minutes, and the source of the odour seemed to be concentrated in a small area above the bed. They told us that they were unnerved by the experience, but then reassured themselves by reasoning that ghosts don't have a smell. I was quick to burst their bubble of complacency by pointing out that in fact they do, and that it's quite a common way for ghosts to manifest. Their faces dropped and we agreed that, should the smell invade their bedroom again, they would come and get me.

The putrid smell returned the following day whilst Michael was having an afternoon nap. Vlasta was quick to summon me, and we quietly crept into the darkened bedroom. By then the smell has dissipated, and my sister and I quietly paced the room, sniffing the air for any remaining trace of the mysterious odour. Despite our stealth, Michael was suddenly alert, and although fast asleep a mere moment earlier, he shot bolt upright in two seconds flat. The sight of two hag-like figures at the foot of the bed sent him into a panic; in his half-asleep state he was convinced that we were ghosts. His mouth fell open in a soundless scream and his eyes widened in horror. His hair was a tremulous grey halo. Vlasta and I burst out laughing, despite feeling guilty at nearly causing Michael to have a heart attack. For the rest of the evening (and indeed until they packed up and drove off the following day) I found myself laughing every time I pictured my brother-in-law's stricken face.

By the third night at Stonecliffe House, I was a little less anxious, despite feeling sure that its ninety-year history harboured secrets and ghosts from its past. It was almost with a sense of relief that I caught a glimpse of one of the resident ghosts, and found him less threatening than I had expected.

I was just about to get into bed when I noticed someone had left a rocking chair at the foot of the bed, directly facing me. I have always had a problem with chairs positioned in this way, as I imagine them to be the perfect position for a ghost to settle in and watch me while I'm sleeping!

I dragged the chair back to its original position beside the desk, and was conscious of someone watching me. From the corner of my eye it looked like my nephew Alex, and I wondered what he was doing up so late. As I looked up to ask him, I realised it wasn't Alex at all, but the ghost of a young boy. He was two-dimensional and washed out, and visible for only a couple of seconds. Less than a minute later he was there again, putting in another brief appearance lest I had any doubts about what I had seen.

After tossing and turning for most of the night, I somehow managed to fall asleep, but was woken a short time later as a strong perfume pervaded the bedroom. It was rich with notes of jasmine and rose, and despite being startled, I couldn't help but enjoy the beautiful scent. I immediately thought of Alice Loxton (one of the original owners) and told myself, *I can handle this. After all, how can such a lovely smell be scary?*

Just as I reassured myself and started drifting back to sleep, I heard it...breathing. Steady and slow, it was right beside me, and I felt the gentle waft of breath brushing against my face. I reached around in the darkness, hoping that it was Stuart. But I knew full well that he was behind me and the breath belonged to someone else. Now I was terrified, and berated myself for regressing to my old feelings of overwhelming fear. Needless to say, I slept fitfully until dawn, pressed right up against my husband despite the vastness of the king-sized bed.

Upon our return to Perth, I e-mailed Jan, the current owner of Stonecliffe House, and asked her if any of her previous houseguests had mentioned that the house was haunted. She told me there had been some murmurs, and that the guestbook did indeed contain occasional references to ghostly encounters. She also told me that Samuel Loxton had died in the small bedroom upstairs, and I was thankful that I wasn't aware of this whilst we were staying there.

Despite feeling so frightened that I wanted to leave Stonecliffe House a day early, now that I look back on our stay, I can't say that I felt threatened in any way. Perhaps I still carry a knot of deeply rooted fear as a legacy of my years spent living in Kensington. It disappoints me, as I thought I had left my fears behind me. Yet with very little provocation they

This shot was taken at Stonecliffe House in Albany...very, very creepy. There is a figure visible on the upper balcony, to the left of the shot. It appears as though a matronly-looking woman in Victorian dress is looking out to sea. Going by the historical photos displayed in the house, I believe the apparition to be that of Alice Loxton, who made her presence known to me by her perfume and by breathing in my face. This photo still gives me the chills!

spring up and confront me, and all at once I revert to being the petrified girl I once was, trembling beneath the sheets.

For a while it baffled me why some encounters with spirits are uplifting and life-affirming whilst others leave me terrified. After considerable thought on the subject, I've come to the conclusion that it's not spirits that I have a problem with, it's ghosts. And I still have some work to do before I can completely shake my fears.

The more I experience of life, and the more people I talk to, the more I realise that paranormal encounters are not as rare as we might think. I suppose that once people become aware of my long history of clairvoyant experiences, they feel more comfortable sharing their own stories of contact with the other side. As such, I have had the privilege of hearing about some thrilling encounters over the years, the most memorable of which I would like to share in the forthcoming chapters.

Chapter Fourteen

Vlasta

Although my sister, Vlasta, wouldn't consider herself to be a clairvoyant, she is certainly no stranger to paranormal phenomena. Whilst her encounters with ghosts are infrequent, when she sees them they are extremely vivid and usually appear as solid, three-dimensional beings. Unlike the filmy figures that populate my clairvoyant visions, Vlasta's ghosts are often hard to distinguish from the living, and their visits usually begin with the belief that there is an intruder in her home.

One memorable encounter took place on a cool autumn night as Vlasta was woken by the feeling that someone was in her bedroom. It was after midnight and her husband had yet to come to bed, so at first she thought it was just Michael. She waited for the familiar weight of her husband to fall into bed beside her, but when he failed to do so, she began to

My beautiful big sister, Vlasta, and I. Taken during our eventful stay in Albany.

feel uneasy. Her eyes bored into the darkness as she scanned the bedroom, straining to see in the feeble glow cast by the streetlight outside her window.

Just as she reassured herself that no one was there, she suddenly saw him: a young, dishevelled man standing no more than a few feet away. He was unshaven with dirty blonde hair, and was dressed in jeans and a denim jacket. Convinced that the man had broken in, Vlasta tried to scream but barely managed a whimper.

As her eyes locked with those of the young man, it dawned on her that she was looking at a ghost. She inexplicably knew that his name was Martin and that he had been killed in a motorcycle accident. He looked just as frightened as she was, and it seemed as though he was beseeching her for help.

By now Vlasta was terrified, and mustered up every ounce of effort to call out to her husband. She managed a pitiful shriek, just loud enough for Michael to hear in the next room. In the few seconds it took for him to reach her, Vlasta's eyes stayed fixed on the young man as he rapidly faded from sight. He was gone in a matter of seconds, just long enough for Vlasta to register his look of devastation. In that instant she felt as though she had let him down, and knew that he had come to her for help.

Vlasta believes Martin was killed not long before he appeared to her, and was probably shocked by his sudden death. Perhaps he didn't realise he was dead at all. She told me that over the years she has often thought of him, and wishes she'd reacted differently.

"He looked so sad when I screamed," she said. "If only I could have helped him."

But fear is a powerful thing, and I daresay there are very few of us who would not react in the same way when confronted by a ghost standing by our bed!

Barely a week after Martin's visit, Vlasta was visited by a ghost once again, this time a small child. Most mothers will relate to a *sixth sense* as far as their children are concerned, and often *feel* their child standing next to the bed before actually opening their eyes to see them. It was this feeling of being watched that roused Vlasta from her sleep, and she was convinced that her four-year-old son Nick was standing beside her. As she slowly opened her eyes, her first thought was *Why is he standing on a crate?*, as he appeared a good head taller than his usual height.

The answer was soon apparent as she realised it was not Nick at all, but a blonde-haired little girl wearing a pink dressing gown. With the haziness of being half-asleep, Vlasta wondered what such a young child was doing in a stranger's bedroom in the middle of the night. As she stared at the little girl, who was standing no more than an arm's length away, she realised that she was once again being visited by a ghost. Before she could stop herself, she let out a terrified scream. It is hard to know who was more frightened, Vlasta or the little girl, who of course quickly disappeared.

Like my sister, I have done my fair share of screaming over the years, but happily those occasions are fading into distant memories. I am certain that the more frequently one sees ghosts and spirits, the more desensitized one becomes, until eventually the disembodied become an expected inclusion in the landscape of life. When I recall how terrified I was at the prospect of seeing spirits as recently as ten years ago, I am so relieved to have progressed to the point I am now. Experiences that would have once sent me cowering now leave me feeling happy, as every time I see a spirit I am reminded that we are so much more than merely flesh and blood.

The Lady and Louise

Louise is one of my oldest friends, and together with our mutual best friend, Kerry, we form a close trio. We have been best friends since Kerry and Louise were in their third year of high school, a pair of mischievous tearaways at a strict Catholic college. I suspect that being three years their senior and an eighteen-year-old university student gave me instant status, and soon after meeting we became the closest of friends.

Having been an occasional (and somewhat reluctant) sleepover guest at my house in Kensington, Kerry experienced the haunting there firsthand. Although she never stayed the night, Louise was well aware of the disturbances that frequented my childhood home. As such, neither Kerry nor Louise was a stranger to ghostly activity, though it was some years before they had paranormal encounters of their own.

Kerry was visited by a dear friend who passed away as she awoke one night to feel his presence beside her on the bed. The visitation was fleeting yet terrifying, but looking back now she feels it was a well-intentioned farewell.

Louise's experience was more drawn out, as a persistent ghost tried to make itself known to her. The way Louise tells it, it was a subtle build-up in attention that persisted until she eventually moved out.

In 2001, Louise moved into a small 1940s house in Mount Lawley, a well-to-do suburb on the outskirts of Perth renowned for its tree-lined streets and beautiful old homes. The house had only two bedrooms, but with its polished floors, claw-foot bath, and federation-style character, it was the perfect haven for a single career woman. It was owned by Louise's friend Janelle, who was living overseas at the time.

It didn't take long before Louise felt as though she wasn't living alone, as she frequently glimpsed a figure at the periphery of her vision. The figure seemed to linger in two particular corners of the house, one in Louise's bedroom near the door and the other in the lounge room. Louise felt as though someone was keeping an eye on her and felt only slightly uncomfortable.

One night, however, Louise went to bed feeling upset, and was crying as she buried herself under the covers. As always, she was aware of the presence in the corner, but suddenly the figure advanced and was standing right beside her. Louise's fear overtook her sadness as she quickly turned on the light, terrified by the knowledge that someone was in the room. In typically amusing Louise fashion, she reasoned that if she set up the pedestal fan beside the bed, it would blow away any ghostly apparitions. As such, she took to sleeping with the fan constantly buzzing by her bedside!

As the weeks went by, Louise soon came to notice that the ghost's presence was particularly noticeable when she was upset. She felt as though it was trying to comfort her. On many occasions Louise found herself cowering under the bedclothes chanting "I'm happy! I'm happy!" in an effort to convince the ghost that she was fine and encourage it go away. But the ghost was insistent, and if anything its presence became more apparent as the weeks went by.

One afternoon, Louise confided in her friend Dawn, telling her that something was definitely amiss in Janelle's house. Dawn was also friends with Janelle, and as Louise recounted some of her frightening experiences in the house, Dawn began to look decidedly uncomfortable.

After some hesitation, Dawn had no choice but to speak. "Well, Janelle did hear something from the neighbours but she thought it was best not to tell you. She didn't want to scare you."

She paused, still uncertain as to whether she should reveal Janelle's secret. But now that she had started, Louise was adamant that Dawn reveal as much as she knew.

Dawn took a deep breath, unsure how her revelation would be received. "The neighbours said that the lady who used to live there committed suicide. She gassed herself in the garage because she found out her husband was cheating on her…"

Whilst she was grateful to Dawn for telling her, Louise was furious with Janelle, as there was no way she would have moved in had she known the house's history.

"That's why she didn't tell me," Louise fumed to me later. "She was more concerned about having a tenant than worrying about me stuck here with a ghost!"

But despite her anger at Janelle, it all suddenly made sense. The ghostly lady had taken a protective role over Louise, empathising with her and supporting her in times of sadness. Perhaps she was offering the support she herself could have done with when she was alive.

Louise managed to keep her fears in check and stayed at the Mount Lawley house despite knowing its sad history until she bought her own house a few months later. Although she was never truly comfortable there, she did her best to live alongside her ghostly protector. Of course she did her best to act much happier than she sometimes felt…and made sure to leave the fan on when she went to bed each night!

Lucinda

To lose a child is the one of the greatest of tragedies, but to lose two is unthinkable. And if fate could deal out a worse blow than this, imagine losing a spouse as well. These are the tragedies that befell my receptionist Lucinda.

By the time I met Lucinda, it had been almost twenty years since her infant daughter Emily had passed away. Emily had been suffering from cancer and died during surgery to remove an aggressive brain tumour. Eight years later, Lucinda's husband, Declan, died, having succumbed to liver cancer. After a merciful reprieve of eleven years, cancer once again reared its ugly head in Lucinda's household, this time as a brain tumour in her fifteen-year-old son Mack.

Mack was handsome, bright, and loving. Together with his two older brothers, he was his mother's rock. When he fell ill, Mack was more concerned about his mother than himself, and would do anything to spare her more grief. He put up a valiant fight for almost a year, but sadly joined his father and sister five months after his sixteenth birthday.

When I first met Lucinda, it had been only six months since Mack's death. Looking at her, I never would have imagined Lucinda had endured so much in her forty-two years; she was vibrant and vivacious.

When she walked into my office for her job interview, I immediately noticed she was being trailed by a tall, gangly spirit. As Lucinda settled herself in the chair in front of my desk, the figure plonked himself down in the treatment chair behind her, assuming the languid pose typical of a bored teenager. He was glowing white and radiant, and I found it hard to focus on Lucinda as I tried to ignore the reclining figure behind her.

Throughout the course of the interview, Lucinda told me about Mack's recent death, and I realised that the young man was there to support her. It gave me a rush of happiness to once again be reminded of how wonderful the world can be, that in the face of such tragedy love had conquered the pall of death yet again.

Lucinda's credentials proved impressive, and her office skills surpassed my expectations. But it was her bright personality that convinced me she would be an asset to my business. I cancelled all further interviews and called her that night, offering her the position. We were both equally delighted as she accepted.

Thus began our year-long working relationship, until she answered the call to support those she could help most and began working for a funeral company. In the year that she worked at my clinic, I was unfailingly inspired by Lucinda's unrelenting joyfulness. Staff and patients alike fed off her positivity, and it was difficult to feel moody when she was around.

As time went on, I realised that Lucinda was highly clairvoyant, and thus was aware of Mack's continuing presence. She told me she was raised in a funeral home, as her father was an undertaker and the family lived on the premises. The young Lucinda never felt frightened in her childhood environment, and indeed it was there that she had her first encounters with spirits. Since they have been a part of her scope of experience for as long as she can remember, she has always felt comfortable with spirits and views death as just a transient event.

In turn I confided in Lucinda about my abilities, and told her of Mack's presence at her job interview. She laughed and told me she knew he was there, but was amused to hear about his typically relaxed posture as he lounged in the chair behind her.

In the first year after his death, Mack was constantly around. He was often sitting in our reception area, keeping an eye on his mum, but it was at home that he announced himself with increasing exuberance.

Lucinda often woke up in the middle of the night to find her son lying beside her, leaning over her in a gesture of protection. At other times she awoke to find the television or computer had turned itself on, usually at a volume loud enough to wake up the household and attract some attention. Another of Mack's tricks was to turn on the shower at full pelt; Lucinda said she could almost hear him laughing as she rushed into the bathroom to turn it off.

Mack's continued presence supported Lucinda through the dark days of early bereavement, nurturing and guiding her as she adjusted to life without her youngest son by her side. As time went on, his shenanigans happened less and less, until he was just a subtle comforting presence, observing from the sidelines. Once he realised his mother would be fine, he backed off altogether, and Lucinda encouraged him to go towards the light. She is comforted by the knowledge that Mack is now with his little sister and father, and she has no doubt that she will hold them all in her arms once again.

When Lucinda left my clinic to work at the funeral parlour, I was sorry to see her go but enriched by having known her, and felt privileged to have worked side by side with her for a year. The patients at my clinic were similarly saddened when she left, but we all knew that she was needed more elsewhere, to help soothe those in their greatest time of need.

Chapter Fifteen

Henry

As time went on, I realised that my clinic was consistently bustling with a steady stream of spirits. I believe that spirits are drawn to places where people tend to congregate, since they thrive on the combined energy of groups. Shopping centres, theatres, and doctors' waiting rooms are particularly attractive, and the reception area of my clinic was no exception.

In addition to the spirits who accompanied my patients, there were others who seemed to come in of their own accord. I often walked into my waiting room to see spirits occupying the empty chairs. It made me wonder if they were old patients who were still caught up in the routine of their regular weekly visits, or if they had just wandered in to bask in the bustling atmosphere of my clinic. I always found these visits vaguely amusing, as I could think of much more interesting places to hang out than my clinic!

I also seem to draw in patients with similar experiences to my own. I quite often find people confiding in me about their encounters with spirits, whether or not they are aware of my clairvoyant abilities.

Henry was one such person, and first came in for treatment sometime in 2001. When I first met him, I thought he was just highly strung, little suspecting the secrets that made him seem permanently on edge. He was agitated, distracted, and often late for his appointments, sometimes missing them altogether. Sandy-haired with a wiry frame, Henry was a forty-year-old, fly-in/fly-out mine worker who lived alone in the Hills home where he grew up.

At Henry's third visit to my clinic, I asked him if he was okay, as he had missed two scheduled appointments in the preceding weeks. His eyes were heavy with purple-tinged bags, and as he handed me his appointment card, I noticed a slight tremor. He assured me he was fine and that he had just been extremely busy. Not wishing to pry, I said nothing more, but it was obvious that something was causing him a great deal of anxiety.

The appointment passed uneventfully, and it was not until I was sitting at my desk writing my notes that Henry began to open up. It was soon obvious that things were anything but fine.

"Any weird stuff ever happen to you?" he asked suddenly. I laughed, unsure where the conversation was going. "Cos, you know, weird shit happens to me all the time."

"Like what?" I asked, and my smile faded as I met Henry's gaze. He looked frightened, and as I looked at him I could see the little boy he once was, vulnerable and on the verge of tears.

"You won't think I'm a psycho, will you?"

"Of course not! What is it, Henry?"

Once he began, the words poured out in a torrent; it was obvious he had been desperate to offload. Henry told me he had lived alone since his father died ten years ago, but now his father was back, and was waking him up every night.

At first Henry would just feel a weight on the bed, very much like a cat had just jumped onto the bedclothes. Over the course of a few nights, the weight became heavier and left Henry in no doubt that there was someone sitting on the bed. Terrified, he'd turn on the light, unsure of the identity of the persistent ghost.

It wasn't long before Henry realised the ghost was his father, as a few nights later, his nightly visitor began to speak to him.

"After I got over the shock, I thought it was all right. But now it's doing my head in!"

He went on to tell me that night after night, the old man sat on his bed, ranting for hours and refusing to leave. He advised Henry about what he should do with his life, bemoaned injustices he suffered when he was living, and criticized the unkempt state of his beloved house. One night when Henry suggested he should leave, his father was furious, reminding him that it was actually *his* home!

For the last few nights Henry had been sleeping in a railway carriage in the backyard, too disturbed to return to his bedroom and the inevitable presence of his father.

"So there you go," he said. "The old bastard is making my life a misery."

Having shared his story, Henry's relief was apparent. He sat back and exhaled, waiting for my reaction. I admitted to him that I also see ghosts and spirits, so I reassured him that I didn't think he was a psycho.

"Tell him to go to the light," I said. "Tell him it's been ten years since he died and he needs to move on."

"I tried that. He reckons he doesn't want to."

"What about white-lighting yourself then? Does that block him out?"

Henry didn't miss a beat at my reference to white-lighting, a technique used to protect oneself from negative energy or ghosts. It simply involves visualizing yourself in a cocoon of intense white light, thereby creating a barrier against unwelcome energies.

"Not really," Henry said. "Maybe I'm doing it wrong, but he's always just *there*. I wouldn't mind so much if he didn't bloody talk all night! The only decent sleep I get is when I'm at the mine."

I suggested to him that it would perhaps be a good idea to get someone in to cleanse his house, but Henry was in a quandary, and felt as though it would be wrong to move his father on against his will.

"I just want him to go to the light on his own, but he's as stubborn now as he was when he was alive."

As Henry left that day, I felt deeply sorry for him. Obviously a highly sensitive man, he was torn between the desire for normality and not wanting to reject his father.

I was not surprised to see Henry's house on the market barely six months later, and hoped that his relocation afforded him some much-needed peace.

A few weeks later, my friend Sam excitedly told me that she and her husband, Rick, had bought a property on Ronald Road, and I immediately realised they had bought Henry's house. At first I was unsure whether I should relay Henry's story to her.

I decided that I should at least give Sam and Rick a warning, as I suspected the old bloke was more attached to the house than to his son. What I told them was met with a mixed response. Sam was open-minded whereas Rick was dubious, but I was satisfied that I had at least told them the story, to make of it what they chose.

I was relieved when they told me they weren't particularly fazed, as they had no intention of living there anyway.

"We're renting it out to Gracie," Sam said. Suddenly I wasn't so relieved anymore. Gracie is our mutual friend.

When Gracie first moved into the house on Ronald Road with her three children, she was over the moon. It was twice the size of her previous house, affordable, and close to the children's schools. She wasn't concerned about its dilapidated state; the kids loved it and so did she.

Gracie's youngest son, Ivan, was the first to notice something amiss. He couldn't quite work out what it was, but he felt uneasy in his bedroom and often lugged a sleeping bag to sleep in the lounge room. Gracie told me that a pungent smell often wafted through Ivan's bedroom, seemingly out of thin air, to disappear just as abruptly.

"It smells like an old man," she told me, "an old man who doesn't wash!"

Ivan was sleeping in his bedroom less and less, until he finally refused to sleep there at all. He told Gracie that he saw two red eyes penetrating the darkness; he was absolutely terrified.

I decided to tell Gracie Henry's story, and amazingly she knew him, and had once even met his father, Mr. Watts. Gracie is the kind of gutsy, passionate woman who will do anything for her children, so she put on her battle armour and marched into Ivan's bedroom.

"Wattsie!" she called into the room. "This is our home now. You need to go!" She was firm but compassionate, as she suspected old Mr. Watts was trying to scare them out of what he thought was still Henry's home.

"Henry doesn't live here anymore, mate, and neither do you. It's time to move on."

The following day Gracie bought a smudge stick, and proceeded to waft its heady fumes into every corner of every room, all the while telling Wattsie that it was time to go. It didn't take long for the atmosphere to clear, and the next time I visited I could feel an obvious change.

I complimented Gracie on her house-clearing skills, as I no longer felt the heaviness of the old man's presence.

"Thanks!" she laughed. "I do feel for the old fella, though. He probably thought Henry was just away at the mines. He probably thought we were squatters!"

Gracie told me that from time to time she felt as though old Wattsie was checking in, but never in the same threatening manner as in the early days. I suspected he had a new-found respect for the new lady of the house, who would do anything to protect her children.

Dorothy

A large proportion of my clientele are elderly people, many of whom attend my clinic every couple of months. Over the course of nineteen years in private practice, I have heard countless interesting stories from my elderly patients, some of which involve encounters with the other side.

One particularly recurring theme is that of elderly people being visited by their deceased spouses, many of whom put in reasonably regular appearances to comfort their grieving partners.

Dorothy and Joe had been my patients for fifteen years by the time Joe passed away in 2007. He and Dorothy were a devoted, happy couple and when I heard of Joe's passing, I had no doubt that Dorothy would be crushed. When I saw her name on my appointment list a few weeks after Joe's death, I braced myself for what I expected would be a harrowing, tearful appointment. My expectations could not have been further from the truth.

When I walked into the waiting room to greet Dorothy, I was surprised to see her grinning from ear to ear.

"G'day, Barb!" she said. "You ready for me then?" As I escorted her into my room, my mind was racing through all possible scenarios. *Did I get my information wrong? Is Joe still alive? Has Dorothy lost the plot?* Feeling totally baffled, I played it safe and simply asked Dorothy how she was.

"Good. Thanks, love," she smiled. "Of course it's all been absolute mayhem with funeral arrangements and all, but now everything's settled down and back to normal." I smiled and set to work on Dorothy's feet, deciding that she was either in denial or had developed dementia since her last visit. I didn't have time to ponder for long, as Dorothy was in a chatty, jovial mood.

"I wasn't sleeping much for a while there. The damn bees in the ceiling were keeping me awake!" she laughed. "But Joe sorted them out for me," she said, her voice suddenly lower. "Barbara, he comes to see me!"

I looked up into her clear blue eyes and I completely believed her. At eighty-four she was as lucid as the day is long, and as she looked at me excitedly I couldn't help but break into a smile. Just in case I doubted her, there was the telltale flash of light behind her, as Joe put in a brief yet vibrant appearance.

Dorothy told me that she had felt Joe around her from the moment he died, often experiencing a comforting feeling of warmth beside her. Smells that reminded her of Joe wafted out of nowhere, and she repeatedly heard their favourite song. Dorothy treated it all as perfectly normal, and relished the presence of her much-loved husband. He had announced his presence gradually at first, but as the weeks went by, it felt more and more as if he had never left.

A few nights before her appointment, Dorothy was kept awake by the recurring problem of bees nesting in the ceiling. The buzzing was relentless, and Dorothy felt as though she would never get to sleep. She remembered how Joe would always get rid of the bees for her, and lay in bed wondering what she should do about them. As soon as she thought of Joe, she sensed him in the bedroom, and then for the first time since his passing, she saw him. He was standing by the wardrobe, youthful, handsome, and beaming.

Dorothy smiled back. She was not shocked or surprised, just delighted, as she had been expecting him all along.

"Joe," she laughed, "you've come to sort out the bees!"

Wordlessly Joe floated up to the ceiling, straight towards the vent above Dorothy's bed where the persistent buzzing was coming from. He drew a large circle of light around the vent, tracing around and around until the room fell silent. A moment later he was standing beside the wardrobe again, smiling his heart-rending young man's grin as he looked at his elderly wife. Dorothy grinned back as he gradually faded from sight.

Elaine

When Elaine first came to see me at my clinic, I little suspected that this vivacious woman would dredge up my most terrifying memories. She had an appointment every six weeks, and as our professional relationship unfolded, so too did the secrets from her past.

Elaine's recollections go back to the early 1980s, whilst she was a guest at her sister's home in Mount Lawley, a sprawling post-war house on a well-to-do street. The guest bedroom was at the far end of the house, nestled in the back near the kitchen and the bathroom.

The first thing Elaine noticed about the bedroom was the drastic drop in temperature, but put it down to the fact that the window was obscured by shrubbery, effectively obscuring the sun. It was dark and stuffy, and Elaine spent as little time in there as possible.

It wasn't long before Elaine began to suspect that the house was haunted, as she felt uneasy each time she walked through the front door. Her feelings of discomfort intensified as she moved to the rear of the house and seemed to be concentrated in the small dark guestroom at the back.

She mentioned her suspicions to her sister, Maureen, who dismissed her concerns with a laugh. She did, however, concede that previous houseguests had made similar comments, but presumed it was just because the back of the house was consistently dark and gloomy.

Elaine's suspicions gained momentum over the course of several nights, as she was repeatedly woken by what she believed was a downpour of rain. Each time she mentioned the rain to Maureen and her husband, they assured her that not a drop had fallen, and presumed that Elaine must have been dreaming. Elaine, however, was unconvinced, so when she was woken for the fifth night in a row, she got up to investigate. The sound of rain was unmistakeable, or so she believed until she looked out the window. The night was calm and clear.

Feeling somewhat disoriented, she walked through the house until she realised the sound she had mistaken for rain was coming from the bathroom, and although it was three in the morning, the shower was running at full pelt. She called out to see who was in there, and when no one answered, she nervously opened the door. The shower was streaming, yet the bathroom was empty. Elaine navigated through the steam and turned off the taps, sickened by the realisation that her suspicions were correct.

The following morning Elaine told her sister, who was also beginning to feel progressively more uneasy as the evidence began to mount. The shower repeatedly turned itself on, and Maureen recalled that previous houseguests had commented on *the lovely night's rain* even when the weather had been fine.

Just when she felt as though she'd had enough, Elaine's impending move to her own home was accelerated by a final ghostly visit. As she was lying in bed one night, the temperature suddenly dropped and a thick stillness pervaded the room. Then, in a moment sickeningly reminiscent of my own experience as a teenager, an oppressive weight fell onto Elaine's chest. For the few seconds it remained on top of her, Elaine was more terrified than she had ever imagined possible. She was mentally screaming for release but was frozen by terror, whilst inwardly berating herself for remaining in a house she knew harboured ghosts.

Later, as Elaine composed herself in the kitchen with a cup of tea, she resolved to never sleep in the bedroom again. She moved out later that week, convinced the ghost had been progressively zeroing in on her as the focus of its attentions.

It was some weeks after Elaine moved out that the identity of the ghost was inadvertently revealed. A letter arrived at Maureen's house, addressed to an Italian man she presumed must have been the previous tenant. Having been left with no forwarding address, she went next door to introduce herself to her new neighbour, and to ask whether she knew the whereabouts of the Italian man.

Whilst happy to make Maureen's acquaintance, the neighbour looked decidedly uncomfortable at her request for a forwarding address. Picking up on her uneasiness, Maureen told her not to worry about it; she would mark the letter as "return to sender."

They made awkward small talk for a few minutes, and Maureen was already leaving when the woman called her back.

"I do know where he is," she said quickly. "He's dead."

"I'm sorry to hear that," replied Maureen, wondering why the woman didn't say so earlier.

"He killed himself in the house."

"Oh…" said Maureen. "May I ask if you know where?"

"He did it in the shower," the woman replied, "in the bathroom out the back."

As Elaine relayed the tale, she and I were similarly spooked as we relived our most frightening encounters with the other side. I was also struck by the recurrent theme of ghosts exerting pressure on the chest area, as not only did I experience this very same thing when I was eighteen, so too did my close friend Dean.

Ghosts gravitate to those who sense their presence, as they are desperate for attention and sometimes will do whatever it takes to get it. This type of haunting is not about malice or creating a disturbance, but is more likely to be caused by a spirit who is trapped and needs help. These are souls who need to be rescued, and rather than fleeing in terror we should be sending them with love towards the light. I would like to think that should I encounter this type of energy again, I will handle things differently from how I did twenty-odd years ago. I just hope that I am brave enough to do the right thing and direct the soul in question towards the next stage of their spiritual journey.

Chapter Sixteen

Simon and Kate

Through the process of writing this book, I have stumbled across countless stories of unexplained phenomena, often from the most unexpected of sources. Ghost stories (very much like ghosts themselves) often jump out and surprise us when we least expect them, as I discovered when I met a business associate for a pre-Christmas drink.

Kate is the proprietor of the local shoe store, and I frequently refer patients to see her for her shoe-fitting expertise. Our respective businesses complement each other, and we have developed a strong professional relationship over the last five or six years.

Kate and I arranged to meet two days before Christmas. We sat out on the deck enjoying a glass of champagne together as we discussed my plans for the year ahead. I told her I was planning on taking a back seat as far as my business was concerned, just for a few months whilst I finished writing my book. Naturally she asked what my book was about, and when I told her, her eyes lit up.

"Do you want to hear my ghost story?" she asked. I was eager to hear all about it, and Kate launched into her account of an experience that she recalled vividly, despite it having happened almost forty years earlier.

Kate's working life began in 1972, as an eighteen-year-old trainee nurse in Oxford in the United Kingdom. Young nurses often develop bonds with their patients as they ease into their roles as nurturers and healers. Kate was no exception, and formed an attachment to a young RAF pilot named Simon. Simon was the same age as Kate, and was suffering from the debilitating Crohn's disease. Kate told me that the treatment for Crohn's disease at the time was nothing short of brutal, and Simon's ever-weakening bowel was regularly resected through surgery.

Kate often sat by Simon's bed during the long night shifts, nurturing a friendship borne out of the most distressing of circumstances. Over a period of several weeks Simon's condition deteriorated, and it soon became obvious that no more could be done for him. He was fitted with an ileostomy, with no hope of a cure. The focus was to make Simon as comfortable as possible, and he was moved to the palliative care ward. Whilst he was no longer under Kate's care, she tried to drop in whenever she had a free moment.

Somehow time got away from her, and several weeks passed without seeing her sick friend. One morning Kate was driving home from the night shift when she spotted Simon standing by the roadside with his mother. She was stunned to see him looking so well.

She turned on her indicator and tried to pull over, eager to speak to her friend and congratulate him on his recovery. But finding a parking spot on the busy High Street proved impossible, so she waved to Simon happily and drove on towards home.

Kate was greeted at the front door by her flatmate, a radiographer who worked at the same hospital. Kate could see by her expression that something was wrong. She was offered a cup of tea.

"I'm sorry to have to tell you this, Katie...Simon's dead."

"He can't be!" said Kate. "I just saw him on the High Street!"

It later transpired that Simon's mother was indeed on the High Street at the time of Kate's sighting, although Simon had been dead for at least a couple of hours. Kate described seeing Simon as solid, real, and corporeal. She is in no doubt that she saw her departed friend.

Kate's description of her friend is consistent with a ghost rather than a spirit who has transitioned to higher realms. Being newly departed, Simon was still very much earthbound, his vibrational energy dense enough for him to appear as a solid being. Ghosts are the souls of those yet to cross over, and for those of us who have the ability to see them, they can appear as solid as you and I.

As for Kate, her sighting offered her some semblance of comfort throughout the years of her nursing career. Simon's gift was a glimpse into a world beyond the painful reality of loss, a reminder that death is not as final as it seems.

Emergency Service

Professions that deal with death can't help but draw attention to one's mortality. Regularly dealing with death can be profoundly depressing, unless of course the professional in question has some sort of spiritual grounding and a belief that we are more than our physical shells.

Kate was fortunate enough to have been shown proof of the soul's survival early in her career. As a result, she was better able to cope when dealing with death in the years that followed.

As any doctor, nurse, or emergency service worker well knows, working at the interface of life-and-death situations can be harrowing to say the least. The incredible highs are pitched against devastating lows, as lives are saved and sometimes lost.

Being married to a firefighter, I have seen firsthand the demands that emergency service work entails, and the emotional toll of situations that result in death. It takes an extraordinary individual to weather these emotional storms, and to give one's all repeatedly in the name of preserving human life.

One such person is my friend James, who as well as being a highly accomplished paramedic also happens to be clairvoyant. Not only does he work at the battlefront between life and death, he himself teeters between the spirit world and our own.

We met in 2002 through James's wife, Liz. It was not long before we discovered our mutual clairvoyant abilities, and frequently compared stories about our most recent spiritual encounters. It is difficult enough sometimes being a podiatrist who sees spirits, but being an ambulance officer with the same abilities is almost beyond my comprehension. The stories James tells me are both distressing and uplifting, as the tragic and the inspiring sit side by side in his daily work life.

The first story James ever told me is the one I remember the best, and took place during a call out to a man suffering a cardiac arrest. Upon the ambulance crew's arrival at the scene, the man showed no signs of life, and James took charge in an attempt to revive him. He was frantically administering CPR whilst his partner returned to the ambulance to notify the hospital that they were dealing with a code blue. James's partner returned in less than a minute, but for the short period that James was alone with the patient, he had an extraordinary experience that will stay with him forever.

Whilst steadily continuing with the CPR, James was conscious of being watched, although he knew he was alone with the man. As he systematically pumped the man's chest and delivered regular bursts of air, his partner was mere seconds away with the paddles that would hopefully shock the man's heart back into life. In the frenetic chaos, James was mentally trying to hurry up his colleague. *Come on,* he thought impatiently, praying that his partner would return in time.

Then there was a sudden hush, and the room stilled and took on a serenity that was in stark contrast to the drama that had been unfolding mere seconds earlier. Through the overwhelming calm James heard a voice, and looked towards the ceiling to where it was coming from.

"It's okay, mate," the man said, his ghost looking down at him. "It's okay, you can stop…"

The man smiled as he began to fade from view and James heard the words *thank you* just as he disappeared. By the time his partner arrived with the paddles, James was simply going through the motions, knowing beyond all doubt that the man had already gone. Strangely, James did not feel the usual hollow regret he associates with losing a patient. He knew that all was as it should be, and it was just the man's time.

Chapter Seventeen

Deborah and Anthony

As far as being clairvoyant goes, friends find it either fascinating or fanciful, some quite openly suggesting that I am either embellishing the facts or deluding myself. On the whole, though, most people have some belief in the afterlife, and are hungry for validation that the spirit world exists. In most cases my friends are eager to know if there are spirits around, and sometimes call on me to check if they suspect there is a presence in their home.

On the other hand, there are some friends who occasionally avoid me, as the last thing they want is for me to come into their homes and confirm that there is a ghost in residence! This was the case with my close friends Deborah and Anthony, who steadfastly avoided having me in their rental home lest I confirm their suspicions about an old man...

You can't be too choosy when looking for a short-term rental property, so when Deborah and Anthony found a conveniently located house not far from where they were building, they were quick to sign a twelve-month lease. The house was a five-minute drive from our own, in the neighbouring suburb of Gooseberry Hill. It was pale brick with a flat-tiled roof, sitting well back from what was one of the main drags of the quiet, hilly suburb. It was tired-looking and had seen little renovation since it was built sometime in the 1980s. It looked neglected and out of place, and stood in stark contrast to its more well-kept neighbours.

The house had been the long-term home of an elderly couple; the husband had recently passed away and his wife had been relocated to a nursing home. When Deborah and Anthony first walked in, they decided *it smelt like death*. They took to lighting incense and burning essential oils, but nothing could mask the underlying stench that refused to go away.

Anthony is a down-to-earth firefighter, a self-confessed skeptic who doesn't allow superstition and emotion to get in the way of a good deal. Deb is my dear friend of almost twenty years, a fellow Virgoan who is intuitive and open-minded about matters pertaining to the other side. They are both grounded enough to have dismissed the air of depression that hung over their new home, telling themselves they would be there for only a short time. Deb's son Zac also moved in, although in the classic style of eighteen-year-olds, he was only a fleeting houseguest as he nurtured his busy social life.

Shortly after moving in, Deb underwent invasive hip surgery, and was rendered a virtual invalid for the next six weeks. She wasn't able to drive and couldn't bear weight for more than a few minutes at a time. Her days were spent reading or watching TV, punishment of the worst order for someone who likes to keep busy and maintain a pristine home!

The days dragged by in her brick and tile prison, and although the musty stench had slightly dissipated, the feeling remained ominous.

It didn't take long for Deb to begin to feel a presence; it began with the sensation of being watched. Shortly after, both she and Anthony began to feel as though a cold breeze had rushed by, almost as if someone had just brushed past them.

It was a cool autumn afternoon when Deb decided to attempt some cooking. It would be the first meal she had prepared since her surgery two weeks earlier. She laboured over a pot of chicken soup, leaning heavily on her crutches. As it simmered, her creation filled the house with its delicious aroma.

Once it was cooked, she left the pot to cool, and headed off to the lounge to reward herself with a cup of tea. It was barely five minutes later when there was a deafening crash. Her heart racing, Deb scrambled for her crutches and hobbled towards the kitchen. Before her was a scene of utter chaos: the soup pot was upturned on the floor, its contents strewn across the tiles. Her impulse was to run, but she was of course helpless. It was obvious something sinister was at play, her unsubstantiated feelings of foreboding now well and truly confirmed. She could do little but clean up the mess as best as she could, and wait for Anthony to come home.

As I well know, being a firefighter's wife can have its drawbacks, particularly when you live in a haunted house. As part of the roster, there are two night shifts every week, the perfect opportunity for bullying ghosts to exert some power.

It was on one such evening that Deb was watching TV when an almighty bang echoed from the nearby bathroom. She was terrified but reasoned that she had no choice but to go and investigate, and hoped she would discover a rational explanation for the noise. Still on crutches, she tentatively made her way to the bathroom. She was met by the sight of the overhead heating light lying in the middle of the floor. Amazingly, it was perfectly intact; not one of its four halogen globes had been broken.

Trying to reassure herself, Deb reasoned that the plaster surrounding the light fixture had simply weakened over time. It was a perfectly plausible explanation, at least until the very same thing happened in the ensuite soon after, sending Deb into a tailspin. She was now in no doubt that they were sharing the house with a ghost.

They were all affected by the heaviness in the house; even Anthony was at a loss to explain the events that had occurred over the previous few weeks. They were anxious and uncomfortable, and were counting the weeks until they could move out.

Oddly, Deb's eighteen-year-old son Zac began to uncharacteristically do chores around the home, jumping up straight after the evening meal to do the dishes. At first Deb and Anthony were delighted, but then became suspicious.

"Okay, Zac. What's the catch, mate?" They were convinced he wanted something. Zac denied any ulterior motive and continued the nightly dishwashing. He seemed more and more stressed, but *didn't want to talk about it.*

Eventually Zac admitted that the old man talked to him, telling him he'd better help out his mother *or else.* This was strange considering the old man had been targeting Deb so far. Was he suddenly feeling guilty?

I didn't know of Deb and Anthony's ordeal until well after they had moved out. Deb told me she purposefully avoided inviting me to the house because she was afraid of what I might see. As long as there was a slim chance of there being a rational explanation, she could cope for the last few weeks until they moved into their new home. The last thing she wanted was for me to walk in and see the old man, confirming her suspicions.

Despite the old man's aggressive behaviour, I don't believe that Deb and Anthony were dealing with a malevolent entity. I imagine the man was feeling confused and displaced, and was expressing his rage at having strangers invade his home. I suspect that Deb was the focus of his attentions due to her vulnerability, but also because she was the person who had replaced his wife as the woman of the house.

Nine months into the lease, Deb and Anthony decided to leave, preferring the calm of their partially finished new home to the ordeal of sharing their rental with the old man.

As they packed the last items from the pantry, Anthony mischievously addressed the resident ghost.

"There you go, Mr. Ghost. You can have the place all to yourself now!"

The words had barely left his lips when the pantry light globe exploded, sending fragments of shattered glass spraying through the kitchen.

The memories of these events still have the ability to make Deb and Anthony feel uneasy. But from the safe refuge of their new home, they often joke with Zac that they will "call the old man" when he isn't so keen to wash up.

Graveyard Ghosts

The graveyard ghost is a well-known entity, but up until recently one I wasn't convinced existed. Why would the dead have an attachment to a graveyard? Surely it would be more likely for them to linger amongst the living, or to remain attached to a location with strong emotional ties?

My opinion on this matter has, however, recently been shaken, and I have found myself reassessing the likelihood that some ghosts may indeed stay connected to their physical remains. My change of heart began at a family gathering, where I was drawn into conversation with one of my sister-in-law Dorina's closest friends.

Anita is a vivacious blonde who exudes confidence. She is well dressed and immaculately groomed, and bursts into raucous laughter with little provocation. I had seen her at numerous parties over the years, but it was not until several years into our acquaintance that I discovered she is a like-minded soul with a sensitivity to spirits.

We were enjoying a pre-dinner drink at Dorina's birthday party when my sister asked me how work was progressing on my upcoming book. Anita's interest was immediately piqued, and she told me that she had no idea I possessed clairvoyant abilities. She excitedly began to ask me about my experiences, and I soon realised that a large part of her enthusiasm was due to the fact that she had experienced similar things herself. Anita and her family live across the road from a cemetery, and the steady influx of ghostly visitors seemed more than coincidental.

One of her earliest encounters took place late on a Friday night whilst, as luck would have it, her husband Neil was away on business. Anita was woken by a thud at the foot of the bed, and her first thought was that her cat had jumped onto the bedclothes. She quickly remembered that the cat was locked in the laundry, and her heart began to race as she slowly opened her eyes.

She immediately realised she was looking at a ghost, and pulled the covers up tightly under her chin as she watched the scene before her. A young man sat at the end of her bed, his head in his hands as he rocked steadily back and forth. He was crying. Anita instinctively knew he was a recently deceased mine worker, despairing at the fact that he was dead. Anita watched him for just over a minute, and rather than feeling frightened, she was overwhelmed by a feeling of empathy. He faded away before her eyes, leaving a sense of sorrow in his wake.

I was impressed by Anita's bravery, as despite my long history of paranormal encounters, I am still not entirely comfortable when confronted by a ghost. Anita told me the scene was sad rather than frightening, as she knew the ghost was oblivious to her presence.

Anita also told me that when her son Theo was a toddler, it was not unusual for him to interact with people Anita couldn't always see. For a period, he steadfastly refused to go inside his play tent, pointing and insisting somebody was inside it. Toys turning themselves on and off were also common occurrences, and as Theo got older, he became more and more frightened.

Although Anita and Neil never felt that the energies in their home posed a threat, for Theo's sake Anita asked them to leave. She stood in Theo's room and spoke out loud, asking the ghosts to move on. Almost immediately, the atmosphere in their home lifted and young Theo's fears dissolved into a distant memory.

Anita laments that it almost felt as though something was missing, as she never felt frightened by the ghosts. Now that Theo is older, she would happily welcome the ghosts back and has made this intention clear. I found myself wondering whether her invitation had been accepted, and arranged to meet with Anita at her home.

It was almost a month later that I made the hour-long drive to the coast, eager to discover whether the graveyard ghosts had started crossing the road to Anita's once again. Anita welcomed me with her usual bubbly exuberance, and I could see why the ghosts would be attracted to her.

She exudes boundless energy, more than enough to share between herself and the odd ghost!

As we sat in the dining room drinking coffee and eating muffins, it wasn't long before the figures began to appear. They were filmy and fleeting, darting behind Anita in what appeared to be a game. I got out my camera and began snapping, but there was not an orb to be seen. I have long believed that orbs are indicative of spirit rather than ghost energy, and as such I was not entirely surprised. The more dense, earth-bound energy of a ghost is less likely to radiate light than that of a spirit, which is a higher-vibration, radiant being. Based on this premise, when orbs do appear, they are indicative of spiritually progressed beings rather than the souls of the recently dead who have yet to progress to the higher realms.

The more time I spent with Anita, the more stories began to unfold, revealing a generous catalogue of paranormal encounters. She recounted an evening a few years earlier that left both her and Neil astonished by what transpired.

It was Christmas time, and Anita and Neil were sitting by the Christmas tree enjoying an evening drink. It had been a hectic day, and they sat quietly, lost in their own thoughts. Upon finishing her gin and tonic, Anita announced she was heading off to bed.

"Already?" asked Neil. Before she had time to answer, a low voice emanated from the stereo, stunning them both into silence.

"Well, you're not doing anything," it snarled.

They were both shocked; the voice was clear and there was no doubt as to what had just been said.

Anita and Neil rarely speak about this experience, and only tell their most trusted of friends. They realise how unbelievable it must sound, as they can scarcely believe it themselves. Little do they know that the phenomenon is more common than they think.

Even scientific luminaries such as Thomas Edison have given credence to the theory of spirit communication via electronic means, as evidenced in an interview published by the *Scientific American* in the 1920s. When questioned about the possibility of using his inventions as a means to establish contact with spirits, Edison responded that he believed it to be possible. He reasoned that if spirits were only capable of subtle influences, then indeed it was more likely that spirit energy could manipulate a sensitive recording device, as opposed to the more fashionable current modes of communication via Ouija boards or table tipping. To this end, Edison devoted a significant portion of his later career to developing an apparatus to establish communication with the subtle realms.

Although its detractors are quick to dismiss electronic voice phenomena as something other than spirit contact, it is prudent to keep an open mind and assess each case on its individual merits. Whilst not providing proof, the backing of great minds throughout history provides food for thought. In some cases, as with Anita and Neil, the proof leaps out at us all by itself.

Chapter Eighteen

The Reassurance of Guides

As I reflect on all of my interactions with the spirit world, I feel extremely fortunate to have experienced all that I have. Although my early encounters were quite often traumatic, they led me to where I am now, and for that I am very grateful.

My clairvoyance has convinced me of the survival of the human soul, and has opened my eyes to the existence of spirit guides, both of which have enhanced my life beyond measure. From the first time I saw flashing lights transform into figures at the Spiritualist church all those years ago, these benevolent beings have become a constant in my day-to-day life, reminding me that we are all surrounded by their loving protection.

Rare is the person I come into contact with who does not have an intense pinprick of light flashing over their left shoulder. When I do not see the flashing lights, I suspect it is because I am not tuned in, not because that person does not have a spirit guide beside them.

I have noticed that certain emotions tend to increase the likelihood of spirit energy being visible. Joyfulness often provides the emotional fuel necessary for the manifestation of spirit guides, but the emotional state that is most likely to elicit their appearance is undoubtedly sorrow. Whenever I am in the company of someone who is upset, I usually see one or more of the person's spirit guides close beside them, relentlessly shining their spirit lights as they radiate love and comfort.

In most cases I usually see little more than a bright flashing light, but sometimes it goes a step further and the lights turn into pale, luminescent figures. I have seen massive protective beings leaning over their charges, and smaller delicate figures leaning in towards the people they are trying to protect. I have seen rotund guides and skinny guides, and every size in between.

One of my most memorable spirit sightings involves my friend Kerry, who at the time was grieving the death of one of her closest friends. As I tried to offer comfort, I was distracted by a glowing figure directly behind her, who gradually became more vivid as time went on. He had a hand on each of Kerry's shoulders, and his head was cocked to one side. I could distinguish his youthful muscular arms and the contour of his hairline, and I could just make out the lines of his close-fitting T-shirt. I was not sure whether the figure was one of Kerry's guides or the spirit of her departed friend, but

I did know that he was there to offer comfort. I remember telling Kerry at the time that she was lucky to have such a spunky-looking spirit looking out for her!

Through my own life's tribulations, I have palpably felt the presence of my spirit guides on numerous occasions, two of which are particularly memorable. The first took place in late 1992, and was precipitated by the demise of my then relationship. My boyfriend at the time had abruptly ended our five-year union (four years as best friends and one year as a couple) and I was left devastated by his betrayal. His bombshell coincided with my final-year podiatry exams, and I was overwhelmed by the pressures of study and my emotional fragility.

I somehow managed to muddle my way through the fog of exams and assessments, and by the time I had completed my course I was an emotional mess. My classmates had organised a trip south to explore the vineyards of Dunsborough. They were planning to relax, get drunk, and celebrate our newfound respectability as podiatrists.

I had neither the energy nor the inclination to go, but knew that if I stayed at home I would no doubt immerse myself in grief and self-pity.

I decided to go so as to spare my parents further exposure to my misery, and hoped that I would be able to avoid embarrassing myself in front of my friends. I joined my eleven classmates on our chartered bus to Dunsborough a week after our last exam.

I was sporadically teary and pathetic; the rational part of me wanted to give myself a resounding slap. I somehow managed to get through half of the first evening's revelry, and was almost enjoying myself when something as ridiculous as a random song assaulted me with memories of my ex-boyfriend.

I was reduced to a sobbing, wretched heap. Not wishing to humiliate myself more than I already had, I slunk off to my bedroom and allowed myself the luxury of releasing the flood of tears I had been trying to suppress all day. I couldn't see a way out of my sorrow and couldn't imagine ever feeling better.

Then, just as I felt as though I was spiralling deeper into my pain, I was bathed in a sudden rush of warmth. I felt completely embraced by love, as though I had been magically dumped into an impenetrable cocoon. I was soothed and I was smiling, yet I was confused by the sudden change in my emotions. It occurred to me that I might well have suddenly lost my mind, but it felt so wonderful to be free of my pain that I decided to lap it up regardless.

I fell asleep smiling, convinced that someone or something was embracing me. The warmth continued to pulse through my body, washing through me like a healing wave of love. The following morning I woke up feeling the happiest I had since the breakup a month earlier, and felt sure that I had been visited by an angel.

Having since become aware of the existence of spirit guides, I believe this was the night that I was privileged enough to come face to face with mine.

I was similarly soothed by spirits some ten years later whilst I was grieving the loss of my third pregnancy. I had come out of hospital a week or so earlier and, not wishing to be alone while Stuart was on night shift, decided to stay the night at my mother-in-law Cate's house.

Eloise and Claire were aged two and eight months, respectively, and the distraction of caring for my beautiful babies was the best medicine a mother in my situation could have asked for. But come nightfall, when my two girls were tucked up in bed, the silence allowed me to grieve for the little one who wasn't meant to be.

I was lying in bed staring into the blackness when there was a sudden flash of colour on the wall across the room. I looked towards the light and suddenly an image appeared, as if a small flat television had been stuck up against the wall before me. The vision was of a woman, and as I watched her tending to her shaggy, dark-haired baby, I realised she was me. I was surprised to see myself with long blonde hair, as at the time I had dyed brown hair cut into a short bob (what Stuart would refer to as a *hair don't!*). The newborn was a robust baby boy, and as I watched myself cradling him, I felt a rush of immense joy. I took great comfort from this experience, as I felt I had been granted a glimpse into the future, and my baby boy would be born when the time was right.

It came to pass that just over four years later (by which time the *hair don't* had reverted to long and blonde) our family was completed by the arrival of our son, Daniel. He weighed in just shy of ten pounds and had a mass of shaggy dark hair, just as he had appeared in the image on the wall.

Rejection and Ridicule

As anyone who claims to have had paranormal encounters well knows, a thick skin is an essential prerequisite for those intending to share their experiences. For every person who embraces the existence of the spirit world, there is someone who rejects it. Carl Sagan's often-used quote that "extraordinary claims require extraordinary proof" rears its head time and time again, yet for those who recite it, no proof will ever be enough.

For those of us who experience the paranormal, there is the constant quandary of whether or not to reveal what we are seeing. Is it worth dealing with the skepticism and the doubt, and the subsequent need to justify yourself and prove you aren't a New Age weirdo? Even in instances where I have produced an accompanying orb photo to substantiate my claims of spirit presences, I have been disbelieved, dismissed, and misunderstood. A skeptic is more likely to accept the highly unlikely coincidence that a dust mite or insect has just at that moment placed itself over the person's shoulder in the very place where I am claiming to see a spirit.

There is also the issue of ignorance to contend with. The disbelievers and naysayers group all "sensitives" under a communal umbrella, little understanding the differences between the various types of paranormal abilities. Clairvoyants, mediums, and psychics are often grouped together, under the presumption that they share the same abilities. As such, I am often challenged on the grounds of not being able to provide information that is expected of me. An example of this occurred not long ago, as a friend was debating whether to hold her daughter's birthday party indoors or outdoors. Rain was threatening and a decision needed to be made. "Just ask Barbie," her husband said. "She should be able to tell you!"

As a result of these ill-informed presumptions, my claims are often dismissed on the grounds of my inability to foresee future events or pass on messages from spirits. For the record, the differences between clairvoyants, mediums, and psychics are simple. A clairvoyant can see spirits (as opposed to a clairaudient, who hears spirits). Mediums are able to communicate with spirits either through telepathy or symbolism, and psychics are able to access information about an individual whether it is in the past, present, or future.

There is, of course, some overlap, and some people are blessed with numerous paranormal abilities. But in my case I am largely clairvoyant, with the odd episode of clairaudience thrown in for good measure. So by all means ask me if your dead grandmother is by your side, but don't expect me to give you details about next week's weather forecast!

As part of the process of writing this book, I forwarded relevant chapters to those whose stories appear within its pages. I did this for two reasons: to gain permission to use the often highly personal stories, but also for editorial purposes, so that those involved could add or exclude details as they saw fit.

I was extremely fortunate that those whose stories I have recounted were for the most part happy to share the validations that their loved ones live on. However, given the emotional content of the subject matter, it was to be expected that at least one person would take affront. This was the case when I approached an acquaintance with the revelation that I had on numerous occasions seen the spirit of his dead father.

It took twelve months for me to summon up the courage to approach him, as I was aware that he was highly skeptical. He knew about my book well before I disclosed its subject matter, and I revealed more and more about my experiences as time went on. Once the seed was sown, I told him that one of the chapters in my book was about an experience I had connected with him, and I e-mailed him the relevant chapter.

What followed was like a slap in the face. His reply e-mail was curt and to the point; he suggested I was being thoughtless. This was particularly hurtful, as I had debated whether to approach him for the best part of twelve months. In the end I came to the conclusion that his father deserved to be acknowledged, regardless of the consequences I would face as a result.

He told me I was being disrespectful to his family and to the memory of his late father. I believe the opposite to be true. To my mind, it would be disrespectful to ignore the presence of a spirit who so desperately wants his son to know that he is by his side.

In the end I deleted the relevant chapter but was satisfied that my job had been done. Seeing spirits is a privilege, one I am happy to acknowledge irrespective of the consequences to my sometimes fragile ego.

At the extreme end of the judgemental spectrum are those who believe contact with spirits is the work of the devil. Whilst stopping short of actually branding people such as me as evil, some religious zealots proclaim that we are being duped by demons whose sole purpose is to trick the living by impersonating the dead.

When one considers the comfort and hope spirit contact provides, the notion of an elaborate ruse at the hands of evil spirits is inconceivable. Why would an evil entity create a belief system that evokes love and positivity? It simply doesn't make sense.

The skeptics and the believers will never see eye to eye, at least not until we ourselves are spirits inhabiting the realms that we can only hypothesize about as mortals. Until that time, the opposing views need to be treated with respect. There is no place for ridicule or judgement from either side of the spiritual fence.

What matters is that we live our lives coming from a place of love, and if that means placing ourselves on the line because of our experiences and beliefs, then so be it. I have never lambasted anyone because of their skepticism, as without the gift of my experiences I might well be skeptical myself. But I similarly do not expect to be derided for telling my story, especially since I come with the very best of intentions.

Conclusion

Where to Now?

They say that life is a grand adventure, and mine has been all that and more. It has been wonderful to relive my experiences from the perspective of maturity, and to realise that the abilities I once considered a curse are in fact a blessing.

My encounters with the spirit world have left me with no doubt that the soul survives after death, and that the bond of love is impossible to sever. It is similarly heartening to have proof of the existence of spirit guides, as I realise we are all more loved and protected than I ever imagined possible.

I have emerged from the first part of my spiritual journey less afraid, humbled, and excited about my spirit encounters yet to come. I'm sure that at times I will falter and revert to being scared, but I will remind myself of the loving protection around me and continue to move forward on my spiritual path.

I refuse to give up on my quest for clairaudience, and have joined a development circle with this goal in mind. Perhaps the scars of my Kensington days are still holding me back, and if so, I need to find a way to heal them.

I am grateful for how far I have come and am lucky to have experienced what I have. We are all spirits having a human experience, and some of us have the privilege of taking an occasional peek into a dimension that is really our home. I hope that with this privilege I can offer some comfort to the bereaved, as I embark on the next phase of this wonderful journey.

If you wish to contact the author or would like more information about this book, please write to the author in care of Llewellyn Worldwide Ltd. and we will forward your request. Both the author and publisher appreciate hearing from you and learning of your enjoyment of this book and how it has helped you. Llewellyn Worldwide Ltd. cannot guarantee that every letter written to the author can be answered, but all will be forwarded. Please write to:

Barbara Parks
℅ Llewellyn Worldwide
2143 Wooddale Drive
Woodbury, MN 55125-2989

Please enclose a self-addressed stamped envelope for reply,
or $1.00 to cover costs. If outside the U.S.A., enclose
an international postal reply coupon.